Gordon Taylor

A Mount Lehman Native Son

THE LIFE AND TIMES OF DOUG TAYLOR

BY GORDON TAYLOR

FriesenPress

One Printers Way ·
Altona, MB R0G 0B0
Canada

www.friesenpress.com

ISBN
978-1-03-917446-7 (Hardcover)
978-1-03-917445-0 (Paperback)
978-1-03-917447-4 (eBook)

1. BIOGRAPHY & AUTOBIOGRAPHY, PERSONAL MEMOIRS

Distributed to the trade by The Ingram Book Company

Table of Contents

FOREWORD

This story should have been written by Douglas Grant Burton Taylor, my dad, as Dad had conducted research, kept notes and planned the writing of his story over the years. Due to his untimely death in 1998, at age 73, it has fallen to me to collate all his notes, ideas and thoughts, and put them into some logical form. Luckily, Dad left a copious quantity of notes and documents. The problem I have had is whittling down all his notes and papers into some manageable quantity such that his story, and the story of our family, is told in a manner that respects his written thoughts, and enhances his legacy, truly remarkable as it is.

I have procrastinated in the task. Should I write this story as if I were Dad, and tell his story as if he was writing it? Or should I write the story as a normal biography? These things I have debated within myself for years. I have decided to treat this task as if I were writing about Dad's life, in the usual biographical format.

I am definitely the second-best person to be writing this story. All of the topics were discussed with Dad over the years, but we don't always pay attention to the details, as some things don't seem to be important at the time. Also, memories fade over the years. Some stories diminish in importance with time, while others remain as vivid as when experienced or told.

I accept all responsibility for the content of these stories, but they are as I remember them.

I would like to thank my cousins Janet Andris and Donna Kingman (and Donna's husband Brian) for lending me their photographs and family notes, including the letters written by Herb, John and Anna Taylor - these are invaluable, and had never before been seen by Dad or me. Also thanks to Gordon Bretelle for his recollections on family members - for me, these added a whole new dimension to family personalities.

Finally, I would like to thank my wife Sharon for all her help in proof-reading, editing and assisting me with word processing. Her suggestions have greatly improved my writing efforts.

Gordon Douglas Taylor, K.C., B.A., LLB,
gstaylor1978@gmail.com

About the Author and family

Gordon Douglas Taylor, the oldest child of Douglas Grant Burton Taylor and Elsie Taylor, was born in 1949. Gordon was raised in Mount Lehman, attending Mount Lehman Elementary School, Clearbrook Junior High School, and Abbotsford Senior High School.

Gordon attended the University of British Columbia, and obtained a Bachelor of Arts (English) in 1971 and then a Bachelor of Laws in 1974.

Gordon has practised law in Mission, BC, since 1974, and from 1978 (to 2019) was a partner in the firm now known as Taylor, Tait, Ruley and Company. Gordon was appointed Queen's Counsel by the Province of British Columbia, in 2014. (This designation became "King's Counsel" in September, 2022 upon the ascension of Charles III.) Gordon is now an associate lawyer at Taylor, Tait and Company. Gordon taught, on a part-time basis, at the University of the Fraser Valley, as a Law Professor, in the Criminology Department, for a period of twenty years.

Gordon and his wife Sharon have been married since 1971, and they reside on one of the original Taylor homestead parcels of land located in Mount Lehman, on Burgess Road. Sharon has a B. Ed. from the University of British Columbia, and taught elementary school for over thirty years. Gordon and Sharon have two children,

Ryan and Karen, and six grandchildren. Our daughter Karen, born in 1976, has three children: Mason, Ella and Evan. Our son Ryan, born in 1978, with his wife Kristen, have three children: Hayden, Lynden and Weston.

Dad's wife Elsie, born in 1925, continues to reside in her home on Taylor Road. She and Dad married in 1947, and, other than Gordon, have three other children: Alan Grant Taylor, Rosemary Elsie Taylor, and John Edward Douglas Taylor.

Grant is married to Carol, is now retired, and lives in the Townline Hill area of Abbotsford. They spend their winters in Yuma, Arizona. Grant was in the insurance business, first, as Dad's associate in his insurance agency, and then as the Secretary-Manager of Mutual Fire Insurance Company of BC.

Rose attended the University of British Columbia, and obtained a degree in Education; she then spent her career teaching elementary age children. She is now retired and lives in White Rock.

My brother Doug resides on the original Taylor family homestead on Taylor Road, in the house originally built by William Burton Taylor and Anna Taylor. (The patriarch and matriarch of the Mount Lehman Taylor settlors.) Doug took over the insurance business operated by Dad. Doug has a daughter, Britney, and a grandson, also named Douglas.

Dad's father, Henry Edward Burton (known as "Buster") Taylor to most, but "Bap" to his grandchildren, was born in 1902, died in 1966, at age 64. Dad's mother, Dorothy Eileen Douglas (Forrester) Taylor (also known as Dorothy Elizabeth (Forrester) Taylor, known as "Granny" to her grandchildren, was born in 1901, in Edinburgh, Scotland, and died in 1999, at age 98. Their other child, Dad's brother, James Edward Norton Taylor, who was born in 1922, died in 2000. Jim's wife, Ellen (McCuaig) Taylor, died in 1987.

Uncle Jim Taylor, and Aunt Ellen had two children; Donna Ellen (Taylor) Kingman, and Janet Elizabeth (Taylor) Andris. Donna's husband is Brian Kingman. Janet's husband, Al, died in 2008. Brian, Donna and Janet, together with Donna and Brian's children (Suzanne and Brian James) continue to farm 80 acres of the original Taylor farm property, located adjacent to the parcel farmed by our family.

TAYLOR FAMILY TREE

Robert Taylor (d 1662) m Joan Weller
Steven Taylor (1633-1665) m Sarah White (1641-1702)
Steven Taylor 2 (1661-1719)m Patience Brown (1680-?
Steven Taylor 3 (1708-? m Bennet Ingraham (1707-?
James Taylor (1747-? m Rebecca Smith (1748-?

William Taylor 1794-? M Lydia Brown; 2nd m Anna Turner
William Burton Taylor (1835-1911) m Anna Reinhardt (1837-1940)

John William (1868-1943) **George Herbert** (1869-1949) **James Edward** (1871-1942) m Elizabeth West

Henry Edward Burton Taylor (1902-66) **Gordon Frederick William**(1908-59) **Katherine Mary Louise** (1906)
mDorothy Eileen Elizabeth Forrester (1901-1999)   m Edward Brettelle
                                                                            Gordon Brettelle mJeanie

James Edward Norton Taylor (1922-2001)m Ellen McCuaig (1921-1987)

Douglas Grant Burton Taylor (1924-1998)m Elsie Wall(1925-

Janet Elizabeth (1946)m Albert Andris (1938-2008)   **Gordon Douglas (1949)mSharon Taylor (1949)**
                                                            Karen Christianne(1976) m Kenneth Berry
                                                            Mason Kenneth, Ella Taylor, Evan Douglas
Donna Ellen(1947) m Brian Kingman (1947)   *Ryan John Gordon* (1978) m Kristen Hahn
Suzanne (1971) (m Dean McKay   Hayden Ryan, Lynden John, Weston Elliottt

Mhairi Ellen (1998) Emma Elizabeth(1999)   **Alan Grant (1959)**m Madeline Hale,2nd m Carol Wickey
                                                            Rosemary Elsie (1955)

Brian James (1974)m Lynn Darling (1975)   **John Edward Douglas**(1962)m L. Edwards,2m P. Yakashiro

Nathaniel William(2013)   *Britney Jessica (1996)* / Diamond Slanina
                                                            Douglas Diamond (2020)

Chapter 1

DAD'S TAYLOR FAMILY ANCESTORS
AND HOW THEY GOT TO MOUNT LEHMAN

Dad was born on May 31, 1924, and lived in Mount Lehman his entire life, except during his war service. But his ancestors had owned land in Mount Lehman for many years before he was born. This is their story; how he fits into it is the subject of future chapters.

Our branch of the Taylor family came to British Columbia in 1887 from Bear River, Nova Scotia. I will detail their travel and settlement here in some detail. The background of the Taylor family's ancestry, from their arrival in North America, is very interesting, and was researched by Dad and me over many years. Dad left hundreds of pages of notes of his research.

Dad was always interested in the family's genealogy, and wanted answers to some fundamental questions, such as:

Where and when did our branch of the Taylor family first land in North America? Since Taylor is such a common name, and therefore difficult to research, even though it is most likely that the family was from somewhere in the United Kingdom, we didn't know where they actually came from.

What became of the other branches of our Taylor family, who remained in Nova Scotia, when our branch of the family moved to British Columbia?

Due to hard work, and persistence, Dad answered these questions.

1. Where and when did our family first come to North America?

Our first Taylor ancestor to live in North America, Stephen Taylor, was born about 1633, and he is first mentioned as living in Cranbrook, Kent, England, where I believe he was born. The first mention of him in the New World has him living in the Hadley-Hatfield area of Massachusetts. In 1661 he married Sarah White, the daughter of a prominent gentleman, John White. The Whites came to the New World from Messing, Essex, in England, in 1632. These family matriarchal roots through Sarah White's family have been traced back to England, which they left almost four hundred years ago. While Sarah's mother and father were born in England, Sarah was born in 1641 in Hartford, Connecticut.

It is a mystery to me, however, as to how our Stephen Taylor (our patriarchal ancestor) came to the New World, and with whom, and until very recently, I had not found information as to his parents. I did know that he was close friends with Sarah's brothers, and it was long suspected that the Whites may have known Stephen's family back in England. That may have been true, but I have now reliably established that Stephen was born in England, to Robert and Joan Taylor. It is still unclear as to how he got to North America, but I can track him there from about 1661, as noted above.

It is well documented how the Whites arrived in the New World; they were Puritans and they arrived on the ship "Lyon" in 1632, with

William Goodwin, and Rev. Thomas Hooker, who were early residents of Cambridge, Massachusetts, and who later became part of a Hartford, Connecticut church, to which the White family belonged. (I am not sure if our Stephen, or his parents, were with the Whites as they crossed from Europe (I doubt it, as Stephen would have been one year old), or if Stephen followed later. I do know that Stephen and two of John White's sons are mentioned in the Hadley-Hatfield area of Massachusetts and, as earlier noted, he married Sarah there in 1661. Our Stephen received a "proprietor's grant" of land in Hatfield, and their only child together, Stephen Jr., was born there. Our relatives from Nova Scotia, Marlean Rhodenizer and her daughter Pat (and their family) have been to the Hatfield property, owned in the 1660s by Stephen and Sarah.

I should mention here that, unknown to Dad, he was not the only one interested in the Taylor family; a distant cousin, Marlean (Taylor) Rhodenizer, mentioned above, born in 1936, and a member of one of the Taylor family ancestors who settled and remained in Nova Scotia, was also conducting research from her home in Nova Scotia. Her branch of the Taylor family remained there ever since our ancestors James and Rebecca Taylor arrived in Nova Scotia in the year 1783. (James is Stephen's great-great-grandson.) In fact, Dad and Marlean were independently conducting genealogical research on the Taylor family for many years before they actually met in 1996. They then collaborated on their findings and have agreed on their joint research, which I summarize in this chapter. Marlean and her daughters, Pat Rhodenizer and Debbie Zwicker, have collectively reduced to writing a comprehensive compendium of research of our families, stretching back to their origins in North America, and England. I have a complete copy of their research in my library.

Back to the story of Stephen and Sarah Taylor. Unfortunately, our Stephen was killed in an Indian attack, in 1665, in a battle which also took the life of Sarah's brother, John. At the time of Stephen's death, their only child, Stephen II, was four years of age.

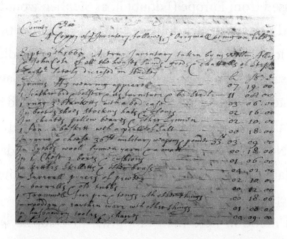

Details of the assets of Stephen at the time of his death in 1665, which I chanced upon, as this was shared by one of our ancestors on <u>ancestry.com</u> The above is very difficult to read, but part of which says: "A copy of the Inventory followes, the originall being on file: Sept 9, 1665, a true inventory taken by Willm Allis and John Cole of all the houses, land, goods, chattels of Stephen Taylor, lately deceased in Hadley. Goods referred to include "wearing apparell, a feather bed, ruggs, blanketts, boots, shoes, stockings, hats, gloves, shirtes…" etc. See if you can decipher some of the handwriting from the 1600s.

As to Stephen II, he married Patience Brown in 1700, in Hatfield. He had four children, but only two, Stephen (yes another Stephen), and Mercy survived. Stephen II died in 1718. His son, Stephen III, born in 1708, in Hatfield, Mass, married Bennet (this is a woman's name) Ingraham. They had eight children, including James, born in 1747 in Bozrah, New London, Connecticut. James married Rebecca Smith, and moved with her from Massachusetts, (perhaps by way of Rhode Island), to Nova Scotia. They likely had all of their land and belongings confiscated after the Revolutionary War, as the Taylor family (at least those parts of it that came to Nova Scotia) stayed loyal to the British, and hence were called "United Empire Loyalists".

James and Rebecca Taylor settled in Granville, Nova Scotia. They are our first Canadian descendants. James and Rebecca had seven children, five of whom were born in the Digby area of Nova Scotia. One of the children of James and Rebecca, namely William, is Dad's great- great- grandfather.

James's wife, Rebecca (nee Smith) was the sister of Joseph Smith, the founder of the town of Smith's Cove, Nova Scotia. We know Joseph came to N.S .in 1783/4, so it is probable that James and Rebecca arrived at about the same time. An early historical record notes that James and Rebecca came to N.S. as "United Empire Loyalists, with two children."

Of the seven children (five were born in Nova Scotia) of James and Rebecca, our ancestor William, was born in 1794. He was married twice, first to Lydia Brown, with whom he had five children, the last of which, born in 1835, was Dad's great grandfather, William Burton Taylor (known as Burton). William married secondly Anna Turner.

Burton Taylor and his older brother James did not get along with their step-mother, Anna Turner, and therefore they travelled to Liverpool, N.S., and went to sea. Burton went to sea as a cabin-boy at age twelve. From family stories Dad heard, he believed that the two brothers probably left on two different ships, as Burton told the family that he never saw his brother James again.

Burton must have, at one time, lived near Fort Annapolis, N.S., as Dad remembered stories being told by the family that he used to play, as a child, in the "parapets" of the old fort.

After Burton married and had his family, they lived in Bear River, N.S. It is from there that the family removed to British Columbia, in 1887. When we visited the archives in Halifax, in 1997, Dad and I found evidence of Burton's family having lived in Bear River - namely, a copy of a receipt for Burton having bought two pairs of shoes back in 1882. They also lived in Digby, N.S. before living in Bear River.

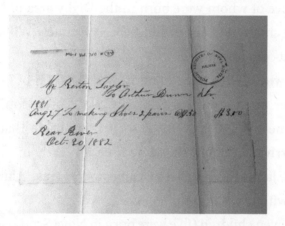

The above is a copy of a receipt which Dad and I found in the archives in Halifax, during our visit to Nova Scotia in 1997. It doesn't look like the shoemaker was a very good bookkeeper, as it seems he made the shoes in August, 1881, but didn't send out a bill until October, 1882!

Burton Taylor was a ship's carpenter in NS in days when wooden ships sailing the seas were the standard. But by the late 1800s, steel ships were beginning to be more popular, and for that, and other reasons, world ship-building influence was shifting from the Canadian eastern maritimes to the British Isles. Men began leaving the east of Canada, and making for the west coast, via the newly completed CPR, where there were new opportunities. Also, according to an interview granted by Dad's father, Henry Edward Taylor, (known as "Buster"), to an Abbotsford newspaper, in 1951, wages for a ship's carpenter in Nova Scotia were then $1.50 per day, but in BC, Burton was paid $4.00 per day.

Dad's great-grandfather Burton married Anna Reinhardt, in 1868. Since Anna's mother had died young, Anna was raised by her grandmother (with the last name of Bangs) in Port Medway, N.S. Anna's mother died when Anna was about one year old, and a sister also died young. A cousin, James Bangs, also grew up in Port Medway, N.S. (More of him later.) Anna was born on September 28, 1837, and died in Mount Lehman in 1940, at the age of 102.

Anna Taylor (nee Reinhardt). I am thinking she must have been at least 60 when this photo was taken. She died on April 27, 1940, at the age of 102.

Until recently, I did not believe that any photos survived of Dad's great-grandfather, William Burton Taylor, but upon recently (in 2019) going through old photos in my mother Elsie's house, I came upon a photo of the entire Burton Taylor family. I am not quite sure when this photo was taken, but according to the ages of the boys, I believe this photo was taken about 1890.

I found this photo in Mum and Dad's house in 2019. I first recognized Dad's grandfather Edward, as well as John and Herb, from other photos I had seen. Later I realized that the whole family is depicted. I made labels to identify each person. I would love to know the occasion for this photo to have been taken- it seems that our family figures prominently in the picture.

The birthdates (and death year) of Burton, Anna, John, Herbert and Edward are as follows: (all were born in Nova Scotia):

William Burton Taylor, October 15, 1835, died 1911
Anna (Reinhardt) Taylor, September 28, 1837, died 1940
John William Taylor, June 20, 1868, died 1943
George Herbert Taylor, November 22, 1869, died 1948
James Edward Taylor, December 31, 1871, died 1942

Anna was a school teacher in Nova Scotia (and her obituary published in a B.C. newspaper said that she also taught in New Westminster). Of the boys, John was apprenticed as a carriage painter, Herbert as a cabinet-maker, and Edward as a tinsmith.

But how and why did the whole family move to British Columbia, in 1887? To answer this question, I have to tell you the story of James Bangs, who was born in Nova Scotia, in 1838. He was Dad's great-grandmother's cousin. He also was raised in Port Medway, Nova Scotia. Not much is known of her cousin James Bangs, except that he was the son of James Bangs Sr. who, as a small boy, migrated to Port Medway with his Loyalist father at the time of the American Revolution. I found, from examining BC Land Title and census records, that James Jr. was in B.C. by 1881, having been registered at "Lytton and Cache Creek, Yale, BC", in census records. There is some evidence that he was working on a survey of the future CPR railroad. By 1883, he purchased 160 acres in Mount Lehman from a George Bellrose, for $600.00. (This is the land, which was pre-empted by Isaac Lehman, one of the founders of Mount Lehman.)

I believe that James Bangs may have been employed with the Royal Engineers, perhaps as a surveyors' assistant, however I have been unable to verify this directly. His address on the Deed of Land, by which he bought the property from Bellrose, is noted as New

Westminster. Family stories record that there was a cabin on the Mount Lehman property; I don't know if Bangs built it, or whether it was there when he bought the property. It was located at the top of a hill on what the family calls the "cabin hill field", which would have been located slightly southwest of Burton, John and Anna Taylor's barn. As I don't believe there were any other buildings on the property at that time, the cabin must have been where Bangs resided.

A copy of the Deed of Land by which George Bellrose transferred the 160 acres of land to James Bangs, in 1883, for the sum of $600. According to New Westminster Land Title records, Isaac Lehman received this land as a Crown Grant in 1878, and transferred it to George Bellrose in 1882.

I do not know where or how, but I do know that Bangs lost a leg, (or at least had a leg injury, which turned gangrenous), maybe in an accident while living in Mount Lehman, or maybe while employed in the interior of the Province. One should keep in mind that, in 1883, the entire property that Bangs purchased was thick with first growth cedar and fir, hemlock and other species of trees. Invariably he must have decided that he could no longer manage the huge tract of land in Mount Lehman. According to family stories told to me by Dad, James Bangs was well thought of in Mount Lehman; apparently the McTavish family (the John McTavish family were pioneers of Mount Lehman, arriving in 1884) had him for dinner on a regular basis, so it seems that he would not have voluntarily wanted to leave the property, or Mount Lehman, but for his health issues.

I also know that Bangs donated a portion of his land, located on the corner of Mount Lehman Road and Taylor Road, on which was built Mount Lehman School. This site has been in continuous use as a school since 1884. See my research on the issue of the establishment of Mount Lehman School, attached as Appendix 1 to this book.

In any event, Bangs contacted his cousin Anna, and her family, in 1887, and offered them the property, suggesting a move to British Columbia. They decided to take Mr. Bangs up on his offer, and made plans for the family to leave Bear River, Nova Scotia, on board the Canadian Pacific Railway passenger train (which railroad was completed to British Columbia in 1885, as a part of Sir John A. MacDonald's promise to link British Columbia to the rest of Canada by rail).

This must have been a momentous occasion for the Taylor family, whose ancestors had resided in Nova Scotia since the 1780s. It is hard to imagine what must have gone through the minds of Burton and Anna upon receiving this offer by mail from Mr. Bangs. Anna was then 50 years of age, her husband Burton 52.

I have a copy of the Deed of Land, dated the 13th of May, 1887, by which Bangs transferred the property to "Anna Taylor, of Bearriver (sic) Province of Nova Scotia", in consideration of the sum of One hundred dollars. The Deed was executed by Bangs in the Township of Malahide, County of Elgin, Province of Ontario, to which area he had already apparently moved, never to again return to British Columbia. James Bangs died in October, 1887, the next month after the Taylor family arrived in British Columbia.

No doubt James Bangs mailed the Deed of Land to Anna after he got the Deed notarized in Ontario. Only a few months after Bangs sent his letter to the Taylors in Nova Scotia, the five members of the Burton Taylor family arrived in British Columbia, with whatever belongings were capable of being brought with them by train. Anna Taylor told her family that the letter from Bangs stated, in part, "It will be a good place for you and Mr. Taylor to spend your old age" -she laughed as she told this to Dad, her great grandson, (obviously after she was over 100 years of age, as she was 50 when she moved to BC.) She then added , "I have lived here longer than I lived in Nova Scotia".Anna Reinhardt's family background was that her father was Leonard Reinhardt, whose father was John Nicholas Reinhardt, which family migrated to Nova Scotia in 1753 on the ship Goehl, from Odenwald, Germany. So Anna's family had been in Nova Scotia longer than Burton's family!

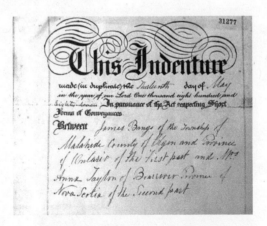

The Deed of Land by which James Bangs transferred the property to Anna Taylor, for the sum of $100.00. Note that Bangs had paid Bellrose $600.00 for the property, resulting in a $500.00 loss upon the sale. Note also the transfer did not include Burton's name.

I have a copy of Herb Taylor's diary, (given to Dad by his brother Jim) detailing the train trip. They started out in Bear River by horse and buggy, and travelled to Digby. Herb commented that they had time to see "their old home" in Digby. Then they took a ferry boat from Digby to Saint John, New Brunswick, and caught the train from there. They then proceeded by train along the St. Lawrence River, until they got to Pt. Levis, Quebec; they then crossed the St. Lawrence River to Quebec City, by steamer, and then once again got on the CPR to continue their westward journey. They left Bear River, Nova Scotia, on Thursday, September 15, 1887, and arrived in New Westminster, British Columbia, on September 25th; in all, a ten- day trip to their new home province.

A photo, taken in a studio in New Westminster, depicting what the family, without Burton, looked like about the time they arrived in British Columbia, follows.

L to R: Herb, Ed, John and Anna

I have Anna (Reinhardt) Taylor's personal Bible.

This is inscribed on the first page of Anna's Bible, namely "Anna Reinhardt, Christmas Day, 1862". This is a very small, non-descript-looking Bible, which I found among Dad's books when I was cleaning out his den. I stumbled upon the inscription by happenstance.

The entire Taylor family, consisting of Anna, Burton, John, Herbert and Edward, were within a kilometre or so of their Mount Lehman property as they proceeded along the CPR tracks to New Westminster. It is not known exactly when they first set eyes on the property, but the story is that they proceeded from New Westminster to Lehman's Landing on the Fraser, just below Mount Lehman, by riverboat, and proceeded up the Landing Road hill, and came upon a young boy. Burton asked the boy where everyone who lived in Mount Lehman was, as there wasn't another soul around. The young boy told Burton that everyone was at a funeral at the Mount Lehman cemetery. So the boy would have shown Burton where the former Bangs (now Taylor) property was located, and Burton, no doubt, would have met all the Mount Lehman folk after the funeral.

One wonders what Burton thought that day. He would have been shown the property, which was heavily treed with cedar, fir, and other growth. Who knows what he was told by Mr. Bangs about the property, but Burton soon learned that there was a lot of work to be done before any of his family could move onto the property. Maybe he stayed in the cabin formerly occupied by Mr. Bangs, until he retraced his journey to New Westminster.

One also wonders what knowledge of New Westminster and its people Burton and his family had when they first arrived. I am guessing that James Bangs must have had many friends and acquaintances in New Westminster (as I said, his address shown on the land title transfer of the Mount Lehman property, from Bellrose to himself, was noted as being New Westminster), so maybe he helped the family with initial introductions to people in New Westminster. We know that Burton was a ship's carpenter in Nova Scotia, and that Herb was a carriage painter. Edward would have been only 17 in 1887, but it is said that he was apprenticed as a tinsmith and also worked as a plumber.

The family, with the exception of John, lived primarily in New Westminster for about ten years. Each of them took jobs to earn money to sustain themselves and to plan for the move to Mount Lehman. They started out as renters in New Westminster; here are some of the entries in the BC Directory:

> "1889, Burton - employee Wintemute, Herbert-upholsterer, painter at Reid and Currie;
> 1890, Burton, ship carpenter, Agnes Street, Edward, clerk at Cunningham, Herbert -cabinet maker, Agnes Street, John - finisher at Wintemute;

1891, Herbert, cabinet maker, 736 Agnes Street, Herbert, carpenter, 429 Columbia Street, John, painter, 736 Agnes Street, W Burton, ship carpenter, 736 Agnes Street;

1892- Burton, ship builder, 426 St. George Street, Herbert, cabinet maker, St. George Street, JW, painter, 426 St. George Street, JE Taylor, salesman, 426 St. George Street.

1894, - Herbert, cabinet maker, Wintemute, res St. George Street.

1897 - Burton, ship carpenter, Occidental Hotel,

1898,- Burton, ship carpenter, Occidental Hotel (he is also on the voter's list in Mount Lehman in 1898);

1902, -Burton Taylor, ship carpenter, 11th Street, JE Taylor, manager, Holbrook House;

1903, Burton, ship carpenter, 11th Street (also listed as such in 1904 and 1905.)"

I also know that Burton built a house on St. George Street, New Westminster, about 1892 (which also squares with the B.C. Directory information). In 2019, I contacted the City of New Westminster, and confirmed that the house, then numbered as 426 St. George Street, was recently designated a heritage property in New Westminster. St. George Street is located very close to the New Westminster City Hall, and contained the residences of a number of prominent New Westminster residents of the time. Most of the houses on that street are designated as heritage houses, and must be preserved under strict rules of the City. I attended at the Burton Taylor house, and was told that the house had been raised and moved to one side of the lot, to make room for another house to be built next door. The

Burton Taylor house has been completely rebuilt, and the number has been changed to 498 St. George Street.

This is the as new replica of the 1892 house built by the family, located at 498 St. George St, New Westminster.

At some point, Burton met Henry West, (also known as Harry West). Henry West was born in Bremen, Germany, in 1835. He was a seaman, and the story is that he went to sea, and somehow his ship ended up off the shore of Washington State. He deserted ship, anxious to join the gold rush, and travelled to the gold fields. However, he was unsuccessful in finding any gold, so he returned to the lower mainland area of British Columbia and/or Washington State, where he engaged in a number of businesses and enterprises. This included a partnership with George Rayberger and Daniel Kilcup, in the wood business (probably about 1858). Later, West moved to Whatcom (now Bellingham) area and secured employment with the Sehome Coal Mines as a superintendent. The mill at the mine burned down in 1873, and the mine closed in 1877.

After the mine closed, Henry met someone named Pickford (or Pitchford as it is sometimes spelled) and established a lumber mill at the mouth of the Sumas River (which flows into the Fraser). They secured contracts to provide timber (either for ties for the CPR, which was being extended to Port Moody, or for dike construction, or cordwood for the steamers then plying the Fraser to Yale.) In the book "Wigwams to Windmills", 1977, in an article by Ridgedale/Matsqui resident Bill Lancaster, he states that cedar planks, 3" thick, and of various widths, up to 3 feet, were cut for the first Matsqui dike at Henry West's mill, about 1876, which was located where the current Ritchie Bros. Auction yard is located near Chilliwack. At some point, his mill partner Pickford suddenly left the picture (some reports say due to illness), and West decided to move his mill to Glen Valley. He apparently put the mill on some form of barge, and floated it downstream to a spot where he acquired property about 1 mile east of Fort Langley. West established his home and mill in that area, where he and his wife, Louisa Falardeau lived, having eleven children. This area, to this day, is referred to as the "West Bluff" area of Fort Langley.

Henry West operated a mill near Fort Langley. It is also said that he established a saloon at Fort Langley. I can only speculate as to how our family became acquainted with Henry West. Our family had lived in New Westminster since 1887, but must have been constantly travelling by riverboat from New Westminster to Mount Lehman Landing. Taylors would have only interacted with Henry West from sometime after 1887 to 1900 (when Henry died), but the interaction between our family and West was extensive. Consider this: Burton Taylor helped West build the flat-bottomed scow the Defender, and probably other West boats, (in fact, Dad said some timber, cedar knurls, from the Taylor property, was used for ribbing for the Defender). The Defender was built with a flat bottom, so that it could traverse shallow rivers to bring timber back to West's mill.

But the other interactions were remarkable; Dad's grandfather Edward meets and marries West's daughter, Elizabeth. Lornie Coghlan, of the Mount Lehman pioneer Coghlan family, marries West's daughter Kate, and West's daughter Mary marries Norton Carter. Norton Carter was injured in a World War I battle in 1916, and was returned to England where he died and is buried. In 1918,

Anna Taylor gifted to Mary Carter the portion of the Taylor property noted in the Taylor property sketch found at the beginning of Chapter 3, (which is a sketch showing the various houses, barns and other buildings on the Taylor properties down through the years.) So Dad's grandmother Elizabeth (known as "Lizzie") ended up living in Mount Lehman, with two of her sisters in close proximity.

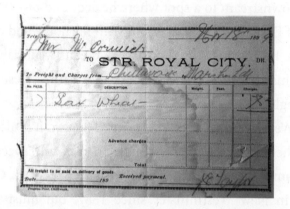

An 1899 waybill addressed to Mr. McCormick of Mount Lehman, for the freight charges to deliver 7 sacks of wheat from Chilliwack to Marsh's Landing on Henry West's steamer Royal City, waybill signed by Dad's grandfather, J.E. Taylor.

In addition to the above, Dad's grandfather Edward becomes the "purser" on one or more of West's boats plying the Fraser, a job he likely held until the time that he permanently moved to Mount Lehman, (about 1906).

As an aside, I found an interesting note in Donald Waite's book, The Langley Story, on the topic of the Defender, West's boat mentioned above. During the 1894 flood, Waite says that John West (Henry's son), who was captain of the Defender, was considered a hero. The scow-bottomed boat was able to navigate through the shallow water and rescue stranded farmers and their livestock. The author also says that the Defender was not the only boat built at the

West mill in Fort Langley. He references that in the 1890s William West (another of Henry's sons) built the Royal City, a boat which took one year to build. This is the boat on which Dad's grandfather worked as purser. To show the ingenuity of Henry West, it is said that William bought the engines for the Royal City very cheap, as the former owner could not make them run, but Henry West fixed the governors on the engines to make them run perfectly.

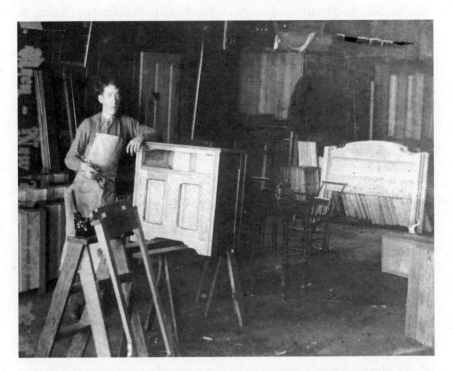

Dad's grandfather, Edward Taylor, born in Nova Scotia in 1871. Here shown working in a furniture shop in New Westminster.

Edward had Nels Olund build his house in Mount Lehman (Dad's notes say that Edward's previous house had burned in 1910.) I am not sure where the burned house was. Dad's notes go on to say that, in 1910, Nels Olund told Edward that he would build him the "finest house in Mount Lehman", for the sum of $2,000 cash (which I believe it was at the time.) This was the house in which Elizabeth and Edward raised their three children, Katherine Mary Louise, Henry Edward Burton (Dad's father) and Gordon William Frederick. More about them in future chapters.

As to Burton and Anna's son, John William Taylor, he was apprenticed as a carriage painter in Nova Scotia. According to Dad's brother, Jim Taylor, John suffered from some health problems relating to ingesting paint fumes, and I think this is likely why John left New Westminster, and about 1893 or 1894, (his obituary says 1893) established his farm on the Taylor Mount Lehman property. The portion of the property to be occupied by John (and later his mother Anna and father Burton) was on the northeast corner of the property facing Taylor Road. I am not sure exactly when either of Anna or Burton moved into this house, however the records of the Olivet Baptist Church in New Westminster give us clues. The records indicate that in 1895, Anna ceased to be a member of the congregation, and that in 1899, her name is again found in the church records. Perhaps Anna moved to Mount Lehman, but later attended that church upon her visits to New Westminster. In the Canada Census of 1901, Anna is noted as "head of the household" and living with her son John in Mount Lehman. See Appendix 3 for a brief history of the Mount Lehman church. (After reviewing the Mount Lehman church history, I believe Anna may have started attending the church upon its opening, which was delayed when a huge tree fell on the church, and the rebuilding process meant that the church did not officially open until March 15, 1896). Her husband Burton seems to have worked in New Westminster for several years after his family moved to Mount Lehman. Burton is listed as a ship's carpenter early upon arriving in New Westminster; perhaps he worked for

Cunningham, (the owner of Cunningham Hardware) who also had a boat building business? Later in the 1890s, Burton worked in the shipbuilding business of Henry West.

Edward Taylor,
about 1900.

I believe that first John would have moved from New Westminster, then his mother and father joined him, at various times, although it appears that Burton kept at least temporary accommodation in New Westminster until about 1904 or 5. It is not known if Burton ever personally farmed in Mount Lehman, but he died in Mount Lehman, in 1911. His obituary says he spent the last ten years of his life living in Mount Lehman.

No doubt building the barn and house was a family effort. Dad told me that Burton had particular skill in crafting timber beams, which were used to construct the first barn on the property. Dad also told me that Burton's ability to cut and square timbers with a broadaxe was legendary. I believe the barn and the first portion of the house were constructed about 1894. This would also square with the date of the commencement of the building of Mount Lehman Church, the beams for which, it is said, were also hand-hewed by Burton Taylor. To this date, the beams continue to hold up the church structure.

The original Taylor house, now described as 30004 Taylor Road, is still standing and is in good condition. The old barn, being the first barn on the Taylor property, was demolished in the 1980s. I have one of the longest hand-hewed beams from that barn prominently displayed at my Burgess Road property (some 55 feet in length). Occupants of that original house over the years have included:

- John, Anna and Burton Taylor; (1894-1943)
- Henry (Buster) and Dorothy Taylor, (approximately 1943-1953)
- Gordon, Sharon, Karen and Ryan Taylor (1971-1980)
- Grant and Carol Taylor (with Carol's two boys, Mike and Chris) (1980-2015)
- Doug Taylor Jr. (2015 to the present).

As to Herb Taylor, the B.C. Directory lists his work history in New Westminster. About 1900, he sought work in the Kootenay area of BC and in fact I have found his name in the census of 1901 in that area. I believe he was there for a few years, following which he returned to build a barn and house on property directly west and adjacent to the former Bangs property, a property called by the family the "Rogers" property, (in letters to each other) where he lived until his death in 1948. I believe this is the property granted by the Crown to Isaac Lehman. In a copy of a letter given to me by my cousin Donna, Anna writes to Herb, who was then living in the Kootenays, in 1902, and says she was glad that Herb had gone in on the purchase of the Rogers property, "as John could never have managed it on his own". More of this property in another chapter.

The Taylor Family Tree is included at the beginning of this chapter. It traces the ancestry of our first known ancestors in North America, namely Stephen and Sarah Taylor, from the 1600s to the present.

The next chapter details how Mount Lehman was established.

Chapter 2

MOUNT LEHMAN FROM ITS BEGINNING

A chapter about the establishment of Mount Lehman is necessary, as its history is important to the Taylor family. Members of the Taylor family first owned property in Mount Lehman in 1887 (having purchased it from Anna's cousin Bangs, who owned the property since 1883), and have continuously resided on this property for over 135 years!

Some asked "Where is the mountain?" when they arrived in Mount Lehman, as many of the early settlers were from flatter lands, like Prince Edward Island, Nova Scotia and Ontario. The answer is that the most common entry point to the Mount Lehman area was by riverboat from New Westminster and Fort Langley. Picture your-self arriving at Marsh's Landing (Glen Valley) or Lehman's Landing (the foot of Landing Road), and having to hike up the "mountain" on foot, likely carrying your belongings. It was truly a mountain by many standards. Riverboats plied the river from New Westminster to Yale, so villages sprouted up close to the river. Places like Clearbrook and Abbotsford were not in existence then.

Dad's sketch of the Riverboat Skeena.

Alben (sometimes spelled Albin) Hawkins, born in London, England in 1838, was one of the famous Royal Engineers who arrived in British Columbia in 1859 from England. The detachment of Royal Engineers was sent for by Governor James Douglas, of the Colony of British Columbia, to help manage the great influx of people during and after the Fraser River gold rush. It was explained to London that within a one-year period, 30,000 gold seekers had flocked to the Fraser River interior region. The few British residents, HBC employees, and farmers, were overwhelmed, and sought help from the colonial office.

London's answer was to send the detachment, called the Columbia Detachment of Royal Engineers (a branch of the British Army), to British Columbia. The purpose was three-fold:

1.   To put in place a program of public works, including surveying townsites and building roads;

2.   To guard against the dangers of US annexation, and Indian uprising;

3.   To create a British presence, and promote a British standard of civilization.

The Royal Engineers were responsible for building the 400 mile long Cariboo Wagon Road as well. They were headquartered in Sapperton, near New Westminster, and they were responsible for surveying and laying out the streets of that City, as well as building public offices and churches. They also surveyed lands, produced maps and settled miners' disputes.

When the Royal Engineers were disbanded, in 1862 or 1863, each man was given the choice of returning to Britain, or remaining in British Columbia. As military men, they were offered grants of land. They were also entitled to Crown Grants, as settlers. Alben Hawkins applied for both, and received a total of 328 acres -about 88 acres on the highland of what was to be Mount Lehman, and 240 acres in Matsqui Prairie, in 1870. After leaving the Royal Engineers, he worked as a carpenter and bricklayer in New Westminster for a time, no doubt to raise funds to develop his pioneer farm.

When Alben Hawkins arrived in what was to become Mount Lehman, his first home was an alder log house. He used Matsqui slough to bring lumber up to the edge of the highland, in order to build his house and farm buildings. He also helped build Harris Road, to augment the original roads- Landing Road, and a trail called "Brewster's Trail".

Visualize that the 10,000 acres that comprised the early Mount Lehman area was a vast forest of Douglas Fir, cedar, hemlock, alder and maple, much of which survived a great fire in 1869. It was extremely difficult to carve a homesite from the forest; a log cabin, a shed or two for a team of oxen; a milk cow, a few pigs and some chickens -no doubt this is why Hawkins chose the land he did, containing portions that were partly cleared.

Hawkins took up residence in 1874, and that was the year he erected his alder log house. He also started a dairy herd, and shipped butter by the keg to the New Westminster market by riverboat.

A few extracts from his diary (the original of which is housed in the B.C .Provincial Archives, in Victoria, as is his "Brown Bess" rifle) follow:

> "Dec. 3, 1874 - drove the cattle from the siwashes-cutting logs in the afternoon.
>
> Jan. 15, 1875. Very cold day - northeaster blowing-feed the cattle at the shed - too cold to go on the prairie.
>
> Jan. 24, 1875 Isaac Lehman arrived to start his farm.
>
> Feb. 10, 1875, put up the logs… Mussleman arrived. Fine day.
>
> April 14, 1875. Arrived home. Samuel Lehman and family arrived. Hauling things from the slough in the afternoon.
>
> April 15, 1875. Finished hauling Lehman's goods from the slough. Went over to Turners in the afternoon. Passmore paid back 1 gallon of coal oil. Mr. and Mrs. Douglas arrived. Fine day."

The diary is a most interesting glimpse into early pioneer life. In the beginning, Alben Hawkins landed by riverboat at the head of the slough on McLennan Creek. He used a raft to bring in supplies and lumber - rafting it up the creek to his farm. The entry on December 3, 1874 tells of his already established herd of cattle and that he drove them over the prairie to the area of the current Matsqui Indian Reserve for grazing.

In 1878, Alben married Agnes Anderson, an Australian, whom he met in Mission.

The community grew quickly, and needed a name. A meeting of the early pioneers was called at the home of Alben Hawkins. A suggestion was made by the group present that the community be called "Mount Alben" after Mr. Hawkins, but he, being a modest Englishman, demurred, and a second choice was quickly put forward by Mr. Hawkins, namely "Mount Lehman", after the Lehmans. This name was adopted, and carries on to this day.

Recently, I came across an article about Isaac Lehman, -this article was in the February/March 2022 issue of "The Vintage Car", published by the Vintage Car Club of Canada, of which I am a member. I quote from this article, written by club member Peter Trant, on the subject of "Cars Converted to do Work":

> <u>"A bit about Isaac Lehman:</u>
>
> *He was born in 1846 and said to have been among the 150 Overlanders who in June 1862 set off in Red River carts from Fort Garry (now Winnipeg) bound for the BC interior chasing the Cariboo Gold Rush dream. They restocked their supplies in Fort Edmonton and prepared for the arduous journey across the Rockies. Soon they had to abandon their carts and slaughter their animals for meat rather than starve. By mid September the group reached Tete Jaune Cache where they divided to take different routes to the goldfields. The larger group decided to take the Fraser River and the others ultimately attempted to raft down the Thompson River to Fort Kamloops. Both groups suffered losses of life, however all but six had arrived at Fort Kamloops by October, 1862. Some, perhaps including Isaac, went on to the goldfields but found that the gold deposits*

were nearly exhausted. Isaac eventually headed south and is recorded to have arrived at Matsqui Prairie in 1874, with his cousin Samuel. In 1875 they were the second pair to be granted many acres of pre-emption lands in the area and Mount Lehman was named after Isaac Lehman. He is recorded as being a blacksmith in New Westminster and moving his blacksmith shop to Ashcroft in 1886, where his wagon building and horseshoeing business flourished until about 1908. Ultimately he became an undertaker in Ashcroft, which is about when he bought his new 1911 McLaughlin, which he kept for the rest of his life. Isaac died at the age of 85, in 1931. ...no one seems to know when or by whom the 1911 McLaughlin was converted into a light pickup truck but one could well speculate that it was Isaac Lehman himself... Isaac would likely have had need of a light duty truck in his undertaking business and as he was an experienced blacksmith and wagon builder he was easily capable of making and detailing the high quality pickup box for his car."

A photo of Isaac's 1911 McLaughlin "pick up" is attached on the following page. It would appear that Isaac Lehman lived in Mount Lehman from 1875 to the early 1880s, I believe the property purchased by James Bangs, and later sold to our great-grandmother Anna (Reinhardt) Taylor, was previously owned by Isaac Lehman.

Isaac Lehman's 1911 McLaughlin converted into a pick-up truck.

According to my Dad's notes, the following families populated Mount Lehman, from the dates noted:

Alben Hawkins, 1874

Lehmans, 1875

McCormick, 1881

Marsh, 1881

McCallum, 1881

Merryfield, 1881

Craig, 1882

Dan Nicholson, 1882

Armichael Nicholson, 1882

Capt. Alexander Gillis, 1882

D. B. McDougald, 1882

James Bangs, 1883

John McTavish, 1884

Lee, 1884

Robert Coghlan, 1886

Burton and Anna Taylor, 1887.

Dates of arrival are not known for the following: Ed. Thompson (store owner), Burgess, Ewart, Mackay, Larmon, Leclair, Anderson, Shroeder, McLean, King, Corby and Ross. There also was another Nicholson, who lived in the Mount Lehman area early on, but it is not believed that he was a landowner, and he did not remain in Mount Lehman.

The settlers needed a school, so one was built at the corner of what is now Taylor Road and Mount Lehman Road, on land donated to the community by James Bangs, Anna Taylor's cousin, from Nova Scotia. The school functioned, from 1884, as a church and community hall, as well as a school, and was opened with Ella Coghlan as the first teacher, in 1884. It is the oldest continuously operating school in our district.

One of the first businesses in Mount Lehman was Thompson's store and post office, located at the foot of Landing Road, near the river. The railway on the south side of the Fraser (to be called the "Canadian National Railway") was not opened until about 1915. A rowboat was used daily to bring the mail from Mission, to Mount Lehman Post Office, and by horseback to Peardonville and then on to Sumas Prairie. What is now Mount Lehman Road was a trail which followed an Indian trail south to the USA, and Brewster Trail angled roughly from Mount Lehman School to the Dennison Road (now called Ross Road) Store area and then further along to south Bradner.

There was another trail that proceeded from near the north end of what is now Mount Lehman Road, from the Nicholson and Gillis properties, over to the corner of McTavish and Satchell Roads, and yet another trail that gradually developed from Marsh's Landing, to Marsh-McCormick Road and to Bradner Road. With the advent of the B.C. Electric tram and freight service about 1910, the store at Landing Road moved, to near the B.C. Electric tracks. Burton Taylor's expertise in cutting and squaring timbers was put to good use in moving Miller's store - the store was put on skids, and pulled with a horse, with the help of a capstan anchored to trees. The skids slid forward on the timbers, those at the back being brought to the front, and the captstan was moved from tree to tree. Although the move took 10 days to complete, not a day's business was lost. The storekeeper kept his doors open throughout the whole operation.

The village was booming. Eventually, the village of Mount Lehman consisted of a hardware store, a feed cooperative, two grocery stores, a bank, shoemaker shop, butcher shop, train station, post office and a milk and freight shipping building. Attached as Appendix 2 is the chapter of the 1958 "Where Trails Meet" booklet, containing the history of Mount Lehman, written by Dad, published on the occasion of the centenary of the establishment of the Colony of British Columbia. The chapter contains Dad's sketch of the location of the properties of the pioneers of Mount Lehman up to 1883, as well as his sketch of the mail carrier on horseback. In this chapter is also seen a photo of the flag-pole raising at the new Mount Lehman school in about 1910, which I believe to be the third school on the site.

According to Dad's notes, Alfred Hawkins, (Alben and Agnes's son) the first white boy born in the Matsqui district, was brought into the world in Mount Lehman in 1880, with Mrs. Lehman acting as midwife. Alfred attended the first Mount Lehman School. He worked on his parents' farm, except for a period of service during the First World War, where he served as an engineer in the Canadian Army. In 1930, shortly before the passing of his mother, Alfred sold the farm to buy a 20-acre dairy farm on Olund Road, a short distance away from the original homestead. He married and he and his wife Irene farmed until their retirement, after living in Mount Lehman for 75 years. They then moved to Aldergrove to a small farm on Jackman Road. As Mayor of the

Municipality of Matsqui, in 1974, Dad presented Alfred with the honour "Freedom of the Municipality." Alfred passed away at the age of 99, in 1979, and his wife a few months later.

So (leaving aside James Bangs, who left Mount Lehman in 1887), the first of the Taylor brothers homesteaded in Mount Lehman about 1893. The pioneers listed in this chapter were their neighbours. The first to establish his farm was John Taylor, at the site of the current heritage home on Taylor Road. We know that Anna and John (mother and son) lived together in this home, and that Burton would stay here when he wasn't working in New Westminster. Then, for about the last ten years of Burton's life, he resided in this house with John and Anna until Burton's death in 1911.

The second Taylor son, Herbert, must have resided on and off on some part of the property prior to proceeding to work in the Kootenays (where we know he was located about 1901 or 1902). As is mentioned in the previous chapter he and his brother John acquired what they called the "Rogers" property by at least 1902, (80 acres of which is still owned and occupied by Donna and Brian Kingman, and their children, and Donna's sister Janet Andris.) Herb returned to Mount Lehman shortly after 1902, to establish his house and barn on this so-called Rogers property located directly west of the property transferred to Anna Taylor by James Bangs. The third Taylor brother, Edward, moved to Mount Lehman in 1906, with his wife Lizzie (Henry West's daughter) and son Henry Edward (known as Buster, Dad's father). Two more children, namely Katherine Mary Louise and Gordon William Frederick, were born to them in Mount Lehman. The Edward Taylor family occupied the southern portion of the Rogers property.

The story of the family farming in Mount Lehman continues in the next chapter.

Chapter 3

THE TAYLOR FARMS

Sketch of Taylor property acquired in 1887 from James Bangs — Acquired from Rogers

The previous chapters detail the arrival of the Taylors in British Columbia, and their years in New Westminster. Now I describe the challenges involved in establishing farms on their property in Mount Lehman.

John William Taylor

It is said that John William Taylor, a bachelor, the eldest son of Burton and Anna, suffered from some symptoms caused by ingesting paint fumes, as he was a carriage painter in Nova Scotia, and he worked at Wintemute's and/or the Reid and Currie businesses in New Westminster. So I imagine that John was very keen to leave New Westminster and establish the first Taylor farm in Mount Lehman. His obituary says he moved to Mount Lehman in 1893, when he would have been 25 years of age. Prior to his move I believe the barn would have already been built on the northeastern portion of the property. All the men in the family would, no doubt, have been conscripted to help in this task, under the watchful eye of their father, the master carpenter.

Originally the family owned 160 acres (the property transferred to Anna by James Bangs). But Anna had sold off parts of the property, on the east, (confirmed by land title records) by 1891 (to J. G. Kirks). Perhaps the family needed money to build the barn and Taylor Road house, and therefore sold that portion of the property. Or perhaps they needed the money to build their house on St. George Street, New Westminster, which they built in 1892. In any event, I believe there were about 120 acres available to farm when John pulled up stakes in New Westminster.

John's house (which later became John, Burton and Anna's house), is still standing and in good condition, at 30004 Taylor Road. I believe that John's house was built in two stages: first, an approximately 20 x 20' cabin-shaped structure, with a loft above containing a bedroom, and secondly, a larger structure attached on the east, containing a hallway, central stairway, pantry, living room, dining room, front porch outside, and two more bedrooms upstairs. As Sharon and I lived in that house for nine years, we are very familiar with its features. You can tell that the cabin part was built first, as in that room (which is now the kitchen), in the south west corner, there is a patch in the ceiling to cover in what must have been stairs to get to John's bedroom in the loft. This would have been before the central staircase, part of the addition, was constructed.

Several old photos I have seen of the house show several buildings on the south side, which probably housed a woodshed, garage-type building, and outhouse. No doubt John had some kind of wood-burning stove in the cabin, for cooking and heating. Kindly loaned to me by my cousin Donna is a photo of the house, dated before the addition was made, (photo date probably before 1900). With a magnifying glass, I have identified Anna Taylor, standing in the middle of the photograph. Others in the photograph are probably Burton and one of Herb or John, and the other brother likely took the picture. I don't believe the house was new when this photo was taken; there is ivy growing up the west wall, making it look like the ivy had been growing for a few years.

John, Anna and Burton's house, showing the initial cabin. This photo was probably taken before 1900, before the addition. L to R are John, Anna and Burton. Note the back porch and shed at back.

The barn on the property first farmed by Burton, John and Anna Taylor. I have the main hand-hewed beam from this barn, hewed by Burton Taylor, on display on hangers outside my Burgess Road shop.

As far as the farm acreage was concerned, it was a mammoth task to clear enough land so that it could be farmed. All the men of the family would have assisted. Dad's grandfather's (Edward's) obituary indicates that he logged with oxen in the early days. It is hard for me to imagine how they would have logged off old growth cedar and fir without mechanized equipment, instead hauling the logs out with oxen, or horses, and then using dynamite to blow the stumps. The logging would have probably been started well before John moved onto the property in 1893. First, clearing would have been done for the barn and house sites. To show how long these chores took, I am going to quote from letters (given to me by my cousin Donna and her husband Brian), the first from Anna to her son Herbert (who was working in the Kootenays), dated May 6, 1902, excerpts of which follow:

> *"Dear Herbert,*
>
> *I have three hens setting on fifteen eggs each, and will hatch tonight or tomorrow, and one was only set last night. … I am going to try and raise some hens for you. … Whitey has a heifer*

calf. It has a pretty Jersey head with large eyes but has a lot of white about her body like the mother. ...We have three heifer calves now; sent one to market, and killed crooked legs yesterday - it didn't amount to much-too small. We are getting a lot of cream now. John says our pails will not hold it when Mollie and Flossie come in.

I have been downtown [this would be New Westminster] -paid some money to Cunningham ... your Dad was paid some money, it was only a short job and your father got some clothes he needed, he did not have much money to sport on when I got through.

There is not much done in the burnt land yet, no fencing, but I hope they will get at it now, we have had so much wet weather. Merryfield sent some of those fine blackberry bushes [hard to believe that they had to import blackberry bushes!].

I hope John and you will come out alright with that place of Rogers, he never could take it alone. I think after this summer you will have to work nearer home so that you can take a run up and see how things are going....Well if there is anything I have not told I will tell you the next time. So good night and be a good boy, with love, from Mother. PS your father came up today."

The second letter is from John to Herb, dated May 16, 1902:

"Dear Herb,

I would have answered your letter before but I have been so busy I have not had time. I got the $30.00 all right. ...The Rogers fields are all sown and the grain looks good except the upper ones that have been cropped so much, and I do not know how they will yield. I sowed half acre of wheat where Campbell *had potatoes and it is about 3 in. high and looking fine. We are at work clearing land now and have it done between the swamp and Israel's line and I intend sowing wheat in a few days. We have to clear for potatoes and turnips, we have none in yet. …The cows are doing pretty well now, we are shipping a can of cream every three days, but Smith lost another calf and Whitie cut the end of one of her hind teats and is only milking out of two so we will have to beef both of them. Bess and Dairy are the only cows to come in, we have had three heifer calves since you left, which I am raising.*

I think I have sold the farm wagon and my old buggy as they are bargained for but I have got no money yet.

I have not paid Fred Harrison yet, and we will have to pay $62.50 interest on the Rogers farm. The fruit seems to be pretty well loaded with blossoms; I don't know whether there will be any fruit that will be any good or not.

Ross was down to Westminster and saw Ed who said he had a job for you there for $3.00 per day. …John"

This is the house at 30004 Taylor Road, showing the initial cabin, on the right, and the addition built around 1900.

Such was farm life in 1902. Note that John was still clearing his patch of land in 1902, nine years after he moved to Mount Lehman! John, with the help of a hired man and Anna, farmed the land, and obviously Herb had to work off the farm to help pay the bills, including the interest on the purchase of the Rogers lands. The sum of $62.50 for interest is, of course, expressed in terms of 1902 dollars. But John and Herbert (together with their parents Burton and Anna) had the foresight to realize that when Ed moved out to Mount Lehman, and when Herb moved to the farm, they would need more land so each of them could establish their own farms.

John William Taylor, dressed in his finest, with pipe in hand.

To get an idea of the lay of the farms and buildings down through the years, I have prepared a sketch, which shows the location of each building and barn, the relative locations of the two parcels of property acquired from each of Bangs and Rogers, and all houses later added to the properties, all of which are still occupied by Taylor family members. This sketch, as I mentioned in an earlier chapter, is included just before the title page of this chapter.

Anna (Reinhardt) Taylor

Next, I turn to Anna Taylor. According to the letters I referred to above, by at least 1902 she was taking an active role in farming, alongside John. They had already established a dairy operation and must have had a chicken coop. The letters note that John was continuing to clear land to expand the farm. I believe that by then the house would have been expanded with the addition.

John with one of the Taylor horses.

We know that by 1894, Burton had assisted in the building of the Mount Lehman Church, so it is likely that Anna was attending the church. In her letter Anna seems quite familiar with residents of Mount Lehman so it seemed that she had lived there for some time before 1902. See my notes of the establishment of the Mount Lehman Church, appended as Apprendix 3. For a staunch Baptist, it must have been quite a transition for Anna to attend a Presbyterian Church, which after 1925, became a United Church. See the Where Trails Meet excerpt, appended as Appendix 2, which I believe was authored by Dad, indicating that Taylor was among the names of church contributors in 1903.

Dad told me that Anna had a very strong personality. This seems to be borne out, when you consider that she moved to Mount Lehman to start a farm with her son John when she was over 60 years of age, and by the tone of her letter to Herbert, John and Herb got regular direction from her. Dad said she was quite devout in her religion, and did not tolerate any bad habits or colourful language in her house.

I have been fortunate to obtain some notes about various members of the Taylor family, not only from Dad (from which I have already quoted), but also from Aunt Kitty's son, Gordon Bretelle. (see the Taylor Family Tree, located just before Chapter One). It seems that young Gordon Bretelle, (to be distinguished from his uncle, Gordon William Frederick Taylor, and me, Gordon Douglas Taylor). Gordon Bretelle was born on my birthday (August 16) 1929; he was sent by his mother Kitty to Mount Lehman each year from 1936-1944 (they then lived in Olympia, Washington). He would spend the summer holidays with the whole extended Taylor family. I am not sure exactly when his notes were written, but he provided copies to our family, and these have been very helpful to me in understanding the dynamic of the family.

Lawrence Coghlan, Lizzie's sister's husband, with a white horse team. This is probably Mount Lehman Road, which had many corduroy areas like this.

Gordon Bretelle's comments about Uncle John and Anna follow:

"After I arrived at the farm, one of my first obligations when I went down to Uncle John's was to go down to his house with him to say 'hello' to Great-grandmother Anna, the Taylor brothers' mother. The first time I met her in the living room of John's house was awe inspiring. This very old lady, who was tiny and wrinkled, had pale blue eyes and a stern countenance. She sat very straight on the front portion of the seat on her rocking chair. Her voice was strong and clear when she told me to come closer, and I remember taking short steps to obey. John had told her who I was, but it didn't seem to register at first. Then he said 'Gordon … Kitty's boy'. In a moment, recognition came over her face and she asked how old I was. She would have been close to 100 years old. …as a footnote to the above story, I can also remember that, during haying seasons, in the

heat of August, Great-grandma, even at her advanced age, with the help of Buster's wife, Dorothy, would carry two stainless steel milk buckets to us in the field. One bucket would have small dishes, teacups, a large teapot with hot tea, a tablecloth, napkins and silverware; and the other would contain freshly made biscuits, butter and jam. We sat in the shade of a tree, and enjoyed the very welcome provisions during a break."

And here is a Gordon Bretelle story about Uncle John:

"John was a lovable character - a Bilbo Baggins style Hobbit. He resembled Uncle Herb more than he resembled Old Man. He was short and round. The most notable feature I remember about him was that he had a magnificent handlebar moustache, which was all grey. I remember that I marveled at how he could drink coffee or tea; and eat soup, pies, or cakes, and not have most of these foods and drinks enmeshed in his moustache. Uncle John had two idiosyncrasies, which were brought to the attention of Doug and me by Uncle Gordy, who was always quick to notice such things. The first had to do with how Uncle John drank water. Since there was no such thing as running water in the early days of the farm, each of the four houses had its own well. In order to have water in the house, a manual hand pump would be located in the kitchen by the sink. Rather than having to prime the pump every time a glass of water was needed for a drink, a stainless steel one gallon milk pail would be kept nearby, from which a drink of water could be ladled as was needed. Every time John took a drink of water from his pail the following routine would happen: he would dip the ladle in the pail and bring it to his lips with his right hand; simultaneously, his left arm would move out slightly from his

body, hanging straight down from his shoulder, which would leave his hand at about hip level. As he started to drink, the palm of the left hand would be facing behind him. As he drank, the hand would slowly rotate until, as he finished drinking, the palm would be facing to the front! Doug and I used to go down to John's house after milking just to peer through his kitchen door to watch this unconcious act; and then run back up to the barn, chuckling all the way. Gordy used to say that he thought it was Uncle John's gas gauge, telling him when his tummy was full of water."

"The second idiosyncracy was in part born of good manners, but none the less predictable. Whenever John might be up at Gabby's house, after haying in a nearby field, he would usually be invited for tea and a piece of pie. The pronounced slurping of his tea itself would tickle us kids - though we were early on warned by Gabby not to laugh; but it was after he had finished the last bite of his pie that Doug and I especially had to avoid looking at each other, for we knew what was coming. As he dabbed his moustache and unconsciously smacked his lips, John would exclaim, with sincerity, 'By George Liz! That's good pie!'"

Anna (Reinhardt) Taylor lived to the ripe age of 102, the last 40 years in Mount Lehman. She lived to see all three of her children establish successful farms on the properties the family acquired in Mount Lehman. Her husband Burton joined her in Mount Lehman, initially on a part-time basis, and spent the last years of his life with her in the old family farmhouse. He died in Mount Lehman in 1911. After Burton died, she lived almost another 30 years in the house, with her son John.

I believe this is a photo of Anna on her 100th birthday, in 1937. Apparently the then Reeve of Matsqui, George Cruikshank, and all the municipal staff, attended and brought with them a birthday cake and a bouquet of flowers. The Matsqui Municipal Hall, at that time, was located at the corner of Downes Road and Mount Lehman Road.

The note on this photo is in Dad's handwriting.

CUTTING OATS ON TAYLOR FARM ABOUT 1910. BARN IN BACKGROUND BUILT BY BURTON TAYLOR (ALSO GRANTS HOUSE)

Dad's grandfather Ed, plowing, with the Taylor Road house in the background.

George Herbert Taylor

The three brothers, from left Ed, John and Herb.

This is Taylor Road, looking east from the Taylor farm. Note the Orange Hall in the distance. It would still be a while before the Municipality of Matsqui paved this road.

This is a photo of Uncle Lornie (Lawrence Coghlan) fishing with Ed on the Fraser River.

A photo of Herb taken in 1940.

George Herbert Taylor, another bachelor, worked in the interior of the Province of British Columbia for a time. The letters I quoted earlier establish that he was there in 1902. I believe that shortly after his sojourn to the Kootenays he returned to Mount Lehman to establish his farm. I am guessing that by 1904 or so, he was living on the former Rogers parcel of land. I speculate that there might have been a cabin either on that property, or in the next field west of John's house, in which he might have lived while constructing his house and barn; in any event he built his small house and barn, and later a chicken coop on a location shown in the Taylor property sketch appearing just before this Chapter.

Herb's barn on the left, his house on the right. If you look carefully, you can see Ed and Lizzie's house, which was several hundred metres south, between the two buildings.

What is known of Herb? Well, I know he was the middle brother in age, having been born in 1869. He was a cabinet maker by trade, having worked at that trade in both Nova Scotia and New Westminster. I know he played for the New Westminster Salmonbellies Lacrosse team. I also know that he was quite adept at photography. Many of the photos included in this book were from Herb's collection, and quite a few were taken in black and white, and somehow tinted by him. Other than that, Dad told me he was musical, and enjoyed singing. A 1993 article in the book "The Place Between", produced by the Alder Grove Heritage Society, says that " in the early 1920s, Helena Gutteridge on the mandolin, Carson Lehman on the fiddle and Herb Taylor, with guitar, provided dance music at Mount Lehman Orange Hall. Music was played by ear, picking up the popular tunes of the day. Parents brought their children to the dances, the children slept on benches around the dance floor, coffee and cake was always served at the dance."

What does Gordon Bretelle say about Herb?

"Uncle Herb was a short man. I seem to remember him as being slightly hunched and portly. He had a nose similar in shape to the actor Anthony Quinn in his role in the movie 'Lawrence of Arabia'. He had a soft, but gravelly voice and he would sort of teeter from side to side as he walked. It was difficult to imagine him as being athletic, though I was told that both he and Old Man were good lacrosse players in their younger years. ... Uncle Herb resided in a single room which I still believe was attached to his barn as an afterthought. It had one window which faced north toward his milkhouse and Taylor Road. There was a table extending out from that window and a bench upon which he sat, located between the table and his wood stove on the west side of the room. On the

south side of this room, which could not have been more than fourteen feet square, there was a single bunk bed attached to the wall. The entrance was on the east side of the room -it was a perfect Hobbit's nest. It smelled of a pleasant aroma of pipe tobacco and 'oldness'.

"After milking and washing the milk pails and all the utensils and equipment and transporting the large milk cans down to the transport dock next to the road, with a wheelbarrow, Gordy and I would go up the board steps to Uncle Herb's room for a short while. Uncle Herb would sit on his bench and Gordy would sit on a bench on the opposite side of the table. I'd sit on the edge of the bed. Uncle Herb would carefully load his curved pipe while Gordy rolled a cigarette, then they'd light up. Gordy had kind of a windproof lighter while Herb used wooden matches. There was a sizable stack of burnt wooden matches on his table; and once the stack reached a certain height, Herb would scoop them off into his hand and toss them into a wooden kindling box next to the stove. The two men would sit and talk for a while, and if it was Friday night, Herb would consult his newspaper to see who was playing the lacrosse game that night, and what time the game would be broadcast on the radio. This information would lead to further conversation about the game and its possible outcome. Once in a while Uncle Herb would accompany Gordy and me in our walk up to the house; and join Gabby, Old Man, Gordy, Jimmy, Doug and me at the dining room table for supper; and then settle in the living room to listen to the game. I would be over my homesickness by this time, and fully enjoy family companionship such as I rarely knew at home."

Each of the boys established very similar farm operations; a basic cow herd, some chickens, probably pigs as well, and of course horses. I read some stories about the Lehman family - Isaac was the original owner of the Rogers property, having obtained a Crown Grant in 1881. The grant covered 160 acres, (so whether our family bought the whole 160 acres from Rogers, and later sold some off, or whether they only bought 80 acres, the amount my cousins presently have, is unknown.) The question I have is what was the state of clearing of the property when Herb erected his house and barn? The Taylor family was at least the third owner of this property, so one would expect that some clearing had been done, and maybe some buildings had been built. So maybe Herb decided to place his house and barn in an area already cleared? If he did, he was lucky!

The Taylor properties required massive labour to log and clear the land (leaving aside my musings about what previous owners might have done), because they required cleared land for farming, they required lumber to build houses and barns, and they required some finished lumber to trim the finer features of their houses. Where did they get these materials? I believe they hand-hewed some of the major beams for buildings, courtesy of Burton. As far as lumber to construct the buildings, I believe they would have taken some of their own trees to local sawmills, of which there were several in the Mount Lehman area, to have them made into usable framing and other dimensional lumber. As to the finer finished materials, I believe these would have come from a planer mill somewhere, probably New Westminster, or Fort Langley. In fact, when I was doing some modifications to the old house, in which Sharon and I lived for nine years, I pulled off some baseboard in the living room, and saw this written in crayon on the backside - "Taylor Brothers, Mt. Lehman, *1901*". This is the type of lumber that would have been loaded onto a riverboat and brought to Mount Lehman landing, and then hauled by horse up to our property.

The other type of wood taken off the Taylor lands was raw logs. The size of the old growth trees on our land was phenomenal! The commodity that the family required above all was sufficient funds to establish their farms. How were funds raised? The brothers would cut the huge logs and transport them to Mount Lehman riverboat landing, where they would be loaded onto a riverboat, and taken to a mill, to be scaled and cut and resold.

I am told that a further means of earning money in the early days was to cut firewood to be used in the steam boilers of the riverboats. I am not sure if our family participated in this activity, but Dad told me that our next door neighbours, the Israel family, had prepared and readied 1000 cords of firewood for sale to the riverboats.

1905 Mt. Lehman football team. Back Row - Doug Currie, Norris Burgess, Athol Lehman, Sammy Nicholson, Ed White, Dick McClure, Herb Taylor, Albert Israel, Harry Ryder. Second Row - Angus McLean, Alex McCallum, Lawreny Coghlan. Front Row - Harry Fowles, Jim Merryfiel George McCallum.

Mount Lehman Football team, 1905. Herb Taylor is in the back row, third from right. Note that in the middle row is Lawrence Coghlan, on far right.

The Taylor horses at the Mount Lehman riverboat landing, with a big log being sent to the Haney mill. Note: this photo was taken before the CNR was put through. Note also that the Mount Lehman pier had a storage shed on it.

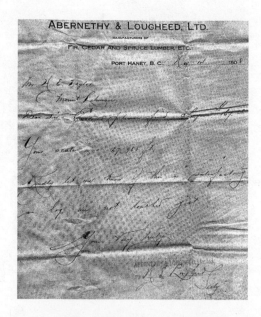

Logging firm account reporting on the scale of 28,000 ft of logs, for which Taylors were paid $167.00 in 1908

James Edward Taylor and Elizabeth "Lizzie" (West) Taylor

I now move on to consider the youngest brother, James Edward Taylor, Dad's grandfather. He was the only son to have married, to Elizabeth (Lizzy) West. I detailed the history of Lizzy's father, Henry West, in an earlier chapter. I want to spend some time, however, to tell a bit of the history of her mother's side of the family, because that is also quite interesting. Her mother was Louisa West, nee Falardeau. It is the Falardeau family I want to mention. Louisa Falardeau was one of the children of Narcisse Falardeau, who worked for the Hudson Bay Company at Fort Langley, as the cook, servant or attendant to James Murray Yale, the chief trader. Narcisse and his family spent most of their time in the "Big House" and adjacent buildings at Fort Langley. According to Donald E. Waite's book, The Langley Story, Narcisse Falardeau was there when Fort Langley was moved and rebuilt a few miles upriver, in 1838. Sometime during this era, Narcisse met his wife, who was from the Kwantlen native band that originally lived in the area of New Westminster where the BC Penetentiary was built. Apparently, that tribe summered on McMillan Island (off Fort Langley). His wife's native name was "Tihepartenate", but was known locally as Ellen. Narcisse and Ellen had six daughters and two sons. Louisa was one of their children. I should also mention that Dad left notes mentioning the Falardeaus. His notes say that Narcisse Falardeau married the sister of James Gabriel (native name "Staquoisit"), one of the hereditary chiefs of the Langley Indian Band. He says that Falardeau was with the Hudson's Bay Company, and was from Sorel, Quebec - coming to Fort Langley somewhere between 1827 and 1838.

As an aside, Dad's notes also say the following: "Henry West married Louisa Falardeau about 1863. They had children - Henry

Jr., Frederick, Charles, John, William, Catherine, Mary, Harriett, Elizabeth, Maude and George. John James Taylor (no relation to our Taylor family) first married Barbara Jamieson, and had one son, John. Barbara died in 1874, aged 33; John James Taylor then married Catherine Falardeau (sister to Louisa West) who bore him another six children. It is known that Henry West built the Fort Langley Hotel and sold it to John James Taylor."

I have previously mentioned Edward, in my chapter about New Westminster. He was the youngest Taylor son, having been born in 1871. He was also the last to move to Mount Lehman, after Herb and John. Ed married Lizzie (as I said, one of Henry West's daughters) in Whatcom (the former name for Bellingham) in 1900. Dad's father, Henry Edward Burton Taylor, was their first child, born in New Westminster in 1902. Edward, Lizzy and young Henry moved to Mount Lehman in 1906, to take up residence just south of Herb's farm. As I said earlier, I am not quite sure in what house they lived before Nels Olund built their new house in 1910, but that new house was quite something.

This house was occupied by Ed, Lizzy and family from 1910 on. Their son, Henry (Dad's father) lived there until he got married; their daughter Katherine, called Kitty, lived there until she got married; and their son Gordon, who never married, lived in that house until the 1950s.

Access to Ed and Lizzie's house was off Taylor Road, up a long lane. (See the previously included sketch of the properties). Burgess Road west of Mount Lehman Road either did not exist then, or did not go as far as the Ed Taylor property. This house remained in its location until the 1980s, when it was destroyed by vandals. I remember attending at this house many times, and marvelling at the woodwork, hardwood floors, stair bannisters, and the beautiful smell of the wood of the old house.

Ed and Lizzie's house - built by Nels Olund about 1910. It was a stately home in its day. This is the home to which Dad and his brother Jim ventured on weekends, to spend time with their grandparents. The people in the photo are not relatives.

Ed, Lizzie and family all decked out in their finery, probably heading off to Mount Lehman church.

This photo shows the landscape of Ed and Lizzie's farm, with the house in the centre, and barn and outbuildings. This may be the original house, which Dad said burned down before 1910. None of these buildings remain today.

A threshing crew, consisting of Lawrence Coghlan, Frank Coghlan and Ed Taylor, at Nicholsons's farm in Mount Lehman.

Once again, I believe that Burton, Ed, Herb and John would have collaborated in the building of Ed's barn, to establish the third farm operation on the Taylor properties, but this farm operation had to support a family that grew to five by 1908. It is this family that I will dwell on for the balance of this chapter.

The Taylor brothers loading the hay wagon near Ed's barn.

The establishment of Ed's farm would have followed the plans previously employed to establish John and Herb's farms, namely to build a house and barn, and then to clear enough land to grow some crops and pasture the animals. I believe Ed and Herb would have worked together closely, with John and Burton assisting, to establish this third farm.

The Mount Lehman Lacrosse Club is shown here, with Ed in the back row on the right, and Herb on the far left. Dad's notes indicate that Ed was the team manager, and Herb the coach. Dad also told me that Herb and Ed at one time played for the New Westminster Salmonbellies.

Dad's grandfather Ed, probably tuning in a sports game on the radio. The Taylor farms did not get electric power from the grid until the late 1940s, (and Ed died in 1942), so they probably powered some appliances by battery. Alternatively, as you will read later, his son Gordon may have powered the house by generator run off a Model T Ford engine.

Lizzie's sister Kate on back left, Lizzie on the right.

I mentioned previously that Herb and Ed played for the New Westminister Salmonbellies. They must have also retained an interest in lacrosse, as is evidenced by the photo of the Mount Lehman Lacrosse Club.

Here are some notes of Gordon Bretelle, concerning Lizzie:

"Elizabeth 'Gabby' Taylor was my maternal grandmother. I probably first met her when I was 5 years old. I think of her today as a kind of icon for the pioneer lady. She was short and stocky, but not overly heavy nor muscular. Yet she could accomplish more tasks in an average day than any modern woman I know! She could put marvelous hearty meals on the table

three times a day. She would wash the dishes, pots, pans and the silverware from each of these meals, seven days a week, by hand, of course, with water drawn from a hand pump in the kitchen. Tending the fire in the kitchen wood-fired stove was a daily task, too, more so on some days than others. For instance, she baked on one day each week, summer and winter - in the summer the heat would be stifling; in the winter, welcome. She baked all the bread for the coming week at one time. Then there was laundry day. With the stove generating near maximum heat, the boiling water would add palpable moisture to the air. Baking and laundry would be done as early in the morning as possible. Ironing would be done in the afternoon; she used heavy individual cast metal irons which would be sitting on the top surface of the stove. With a wood and metal handle, which had some sort of adjustable gripping device, she could alternately place an iron, which was cooling, back on the stove, and pick up a heated iron to continue the task at hand. This was pretty hard work. Then there was canning, in various seasons, house maintenance in a 7-room house, and gardening. … a couple of other things stick in my memory, for example, she smoked, rolling her own cigarettes, of course, as the men did. Somehow, she also found time to paint some very pretty scenes on the white surfaces found on fungus, which grew low on the trunks of trees in the forests surrounding the farm. Some of the fungi were small- maybe 8” wide and 4-5” tall; and some were pretty large - 14” long and 8” high. These painted fungi sat on a small table in the foyer in the house front entrance. Also in that foyer were some early Indian artifacts turned up in the course of working the fields. I particularly remember an interesting mortar and pestle, the pestle used as a doorstop for the kitchen door leading into the foyer …Sunday dinners were truly gastronomical feasts! Meats, vegetables, gravies and sauces, breads, fruits, pies, cakes … all these things in seemingly endless supply. These dinners were not for guests or dignitaries, but were simply Sunday family meals."

Here is another Gordon Bretelle story about Lizzie [this time commenting on her Indian medicine skills, following upon Gordon stepping on a nail, which almost went right through his foot.]

"I was about to get a lesson in early Indian medicine … I didn't know what to make of Gabby's nursing skills. I was very curious when I heard her tell Gordy and Old Man that she was going to put a 'bread poultice' on my foot! With some wadded up moistened bread stuck on the bottom of my foot, all wrapped in some cotton bandage to hold it snug, I lay on one of the two chaise lounges in the kitchen, with my foot elevated on some pillows while Gabby went about her chores. A few days later, she decided to change the treatment. She went outside one morning, and by standing on one leg, I could see her walking around all bent over looking closely at the lawn. Once in a while she'd bend down and pluck something from the grass. After twenty minutes or so she headed back to the house, and I resumed my prone position. She came into the kitchen with a small handful of some little leafy green weeds and a satisfied smile on her face. I wondered what was coming next. … it was to be another type of 'poultice'. I might have thought I was in the hands of a witch doctor except for the fact that I saw the results of her bread poultice as she showed it to Aunt Dorothy and other members of the family who had come to see how I was recovering. The poultice had indeed drawn

some debris and unappealing other stuff from the hole in my foot. Amazing! So I was less concerned about the 'weed poultice' she was going to apply. It also drew out more stuff over the next several days. ...the pain and swelling went down over a couple of weeks, and I was getting antsy. ... Gordy presented me with a really neat and comfortable crutch which he had constructed out in his shop ... I learned to get around very well with it, though I was not allowed out of the yard for awhile. It was the end of August, a few weeks after my accident, when Mum and Dad arrived to pick me up and take me home. In her letters, Gabby had not told Mum about my injury because she didn't want them to worry - and besides, everything was under control. When Mum saw me hobbling about on my crutch, she was surprised and concerned. Over coffee on the front veranda, Gabby filled Mum and Dad in on the whole affair in great detail. After they heard all about it, Mum asked Gabby where they took me for my tetanus shot? Mum nearly fainted in shock when Gabby told her they had not bothered to get one for me! I didn't know anything about how serious tetanus was until I was in my teens. A rusty old spike in a barnyard, run deeply into a foot! Good God!"

My cousins Donna and Janet also tell me that their father (my Uncle Jim) told them that Gabby (his grandmother Lizzie) made a "special poultice" out of an egg membrane one time, to re-attach the tip of Uncle John's nose, which had somehow been sliced off by an axe.

This is my favourite photo of the family - as they looked in 1939. From L to R: Ed Taylor, Gussy McPhail (friend of Aunt Kitty), Gordon Bretelle, Kitty Bretelle (Aunt Kitty), Buster Taylor (Bap), Ralph Caruso (foster child of Ed and Lizzie), Dorothy Taylor (Granny), Jim Taylor (Uncle Jim), Gordon Taylor (Uncle Gordy) and Douglas Taylor (my Dad).

The following are examples of comments made by Gordon Bretelle about his grandfather Edward:

"Edward Taylor - 'Ed' Taylor, as he was known to most around Mt. Lehman - 'Old Man' as he was known to Jimmy, Doug, and me. As far as I knew, Old Man was the patriarch and de facto head of the Taylors in Mt. Lehman. Whatever discussions took place concerning the business or operation of the farms, which I ever overheard, seemed to be contingent on the views of the Old Man. Jimmy and Doug overheard such discussions; hence they started calling him 'Old Man' in very early childhood. I picked up that loving moniker on my first visit to the farm. He was an impressive figure. I don't remember him as being very tall, but I do remember him as very handsome. A striking fellow. His face reflected his occupation; his skin appeared to

me to be the colour of deep mahogany in the summers when I knew him, and was accentuated by his thick, snow white hair. There were lines in his face, attesting to several decades of farming out in the hard elements of the Fraser River Valley weather. He was lean and strong, but demonstrated an air of brains over brawn. ... Old Man had deep thoughts, which as far as I could tell, he rarely expressed. I think he had a strong love and respect for nature, and was pretty aware of its power, logic and beauty. When he could take time from the many tasks of the day, he'd enlighten and teach me of the marvels of nature. One summer evening as he and I were on our way back up to the house after milking down at Uncle John's barn, he paused in the field of growing hay. We sat down next to the trail and he took from his pocket a tin of home-rolled cigarettes and, after lighting one, he laid back on one elbow and proceeded to show me how to find all sorts of marvelous images in the cumulous clouds which were still lit by the setting sun. There were funny men's faces with bulbous noses; snapping alligators, rearing horses; the more he pointed out, the more I could find for myself. Imagination! What a fascinating thing to learn to use! I have used it all my life - and remember to this day who taught me how. ...another of Old Man's skills was raising the most impressive vegetable garden I have ever seen. He was an experienced farmer, for sure, and his family had to have food to eat - not just in the summer, but year round. He grew this produce; Gabby canned it - thus they ate almost as well in the winter as in the summer."

"To see a World in a grain of sand,

And a Heaven in a wild flower,

Hold Infinity in the palm of your hand,

And Eternity in an hour."

(Excerpt from William Blake's ' Auguries of Innocence')

Bap on his horse "Prince". Note the Orange Hall above the horse's ears, and Mount Lehman School peaking out to the left of the barn.

The entire Ed and Lizzie family, from L to R:
Bap, Ed, Uncle Gordy, Lizzie and Aunt Kitty.

Henry Edward Burton Taylor and Dorothy Eileen Douglas (Forrester) Taylor

Dad's father Henry, nicknamed "Buster", born in 1902, and his sister Katherine, known as "Kitty", and brother Gordon, attended Mount Lehman School.

Bap and Aunt Kitty atop a white horse.

Ed and Lizzie's three children: L to R, Aunt Kitty, Bap and Uncle Gordy

So I will start with Ed and Lizzy's oldest child, Dad's father, Henry. I don't know when the nickname "Buster" came to be, or why. I never knew him as either of those names, of course, as he was my grandfather; we called him "Bap", as apparently his oldest grandchild, my cousin Janet, when very young, thought that was how one pronounced "grandad". From here on, I am going to refer to Henry Edward Burton Taylor as "Bap".

I have a copy of an article about Bap, which appeared in 1951 in the Abbotsford, Sumas and Matsqui newspaper, by interviewer E. K. Wilson. I will paraphrase the contents of this article. In it, Bap states that he came to Mount Lehman, with his parents, in 1906, when four years of age. He says that two years later he started his education in a small one-roomed school, where his teacher, Miss Law, struggled with about 70 children until a two-roomed school was constructed after the old one was pulled down. To have lessons while the change-over was taking place, students attended classes in the Orange Hall.

A photo of the parents and students at Mount Lehman School about 1912. Lizzie is in the back row, third from right. Kitty is in the middle row, in the dress with white collars, and Bap is in the front row, fourth from right, with a white shirt and dark tie.

Bap goes on to say that the chief sport, for which Mount Lehman was famous, was what they then called football (now called soccer). Early on a fierce rivalry in football was had between Mount Lehman and neighbouring communities, especially Bradner.

The interviewer goes on to relate that life was active in the district, and that there were several sawmills functioning in the Mount Lehman area, and that Mount Lehman Road was the main thoroughfare down to the river wharf, and Aldergrove and adjacent neighbours used Mount Lehman Road as well. He says that Abbotsford consisted of only six or seven tarpaper shacks when he first remembered it, but it boasted a painted building, the Commercial Hotel.

Bap recalls that Mount Lehman Store was situated near the wharf, and there people came to exchange news of the day, and to bring their cream for shipment. He said he recalled the shipping out of the last team of oxen, which had been the property of Sam Larmon. The store at the river was owned by Henry Alder, who had a complete stock of feed, groceries, clothing, boots and other wares of various kinds -this store was located at the riverboat stop called "Lehman's Landing".

Bap continues by saying that his grandmother's cousin (Bangs) had deeded the property to Anna Taylor in 1887, (and as I said earlier, the Rogers properties were later acquired) and that, as at 1951, Bap and his brother Gordon still owned the original properties.

Bap reminisced about the early days of clearing land in Mount Lehman, saying that when the Taylor family first arrived in Mount Lehman, very few acres were cleared in the dense forest. After the trees were cut and limbed, a mini-railway bed was built to haul out the logs, then stumps were blasted and horses were used to pull them out, as there were no bulldozers in those days. He says the only way for people to earn ready cash was to sell cordwood to the steamers plying the Fraser, earning $1.25 per cord.

Bap comments about men like his grandfather Burton leaving for the west, where there was developing a brisk activity in the building of sternwheelers. He says the time to construct a sternwheeler was 18 months, and that the men engaged in the construction were paid at the conclusion of the building of the vessel. The construction companies had their own stores, and gave credit during the building of the vessel, and adjusted the debits and credits at the termination of construction. So skilled were men with a broad axe in those days that the ship ribs made of hewn timber looked as though they had been through a planer mill. He said that timbers in his barn were hand hewn and bear the unmistakable artistic touch of his grandfather. (The beam I have hanging outside my shop is one of those.)

Bap said that newcomers to the Province of BC in the old days filed on a parcel of property (at the Land Title office in New Westminster) and then generally would find a job in New Westminster (which was much larger than Vancouver at that time). He said his uncles would work on the land until it became necessary to make money to carry them through another phase of building their farms, and then would go back to New Westminster to earn more money.

Bap speaks about Mount Lehman School, saying that before he left school, it had grown from a one roomed school into a superior school, which included high school grades. When he had completed his formal education he went to work on the farm, and then for three years worked with the government department of public works in the area, and was also employed by Matsqui Municipal council for five years in construction work. This work, he says, helped him over lean years when farming was not giving expected returns.

A photo provided to me courtesy of the Reach Gallery, P53 (Abbotsford). Bap is the little guy in the front row, third from right. Mount Lehman School looks very new here, so this was probably taken about 1912.

Another photo of my grandfather Bap, maybe age 14?

In the newspaper article, Bap goes on to say that, in the early twenties, he and his sister Kitty had an orchestra which "played the boards" all the way from New Westminster to Chilliwack. He played the saxophone and his sister played the piano. Another member of the band was Jessie Coogan with her violin. There were additional members and additional instruments as the occasion demanded. He says that in those days, travel was not easy, on gravel roads mostly, and there were constant flat tires on his vehicles; the tire and tube had to be removed from the wheel, patched, and re-installed, causing some delays.

Bap, with his grandfather Burton.
Bap is fishing and Burton is holding a brace of birds.

It is obvious from Bap's comments in the news article that he loved the MSA district, and he says "there is just no place like the Fraser Valley". He goes on to say that today (this would be 1951) from almost any farm in the Mount Lehman district, there comes as much produce as came from the whole district when he was a child, as farming methods have been greatly improved.

Bap went on to talk about taking part in the community; he says he has been a member of Mount Lehman Orange Lodge No. 1868,

Bap, dressed in a boy-scout type uniform, on the Taylor property. Note the size of the trees surrounding him.

founded in September 1904, for thirty years. He outlined that he has been master of the local organization and was county master of Chilliwack county in 1946. He then went on to detail his war involvement; when money was required to fund World War II efforts, Bap sold what were called "victory loans," and said he was the only salesman who worked through nine "campaigns" to sell them. He said he received a certificate from the government for the work he did in the county districts and his volume of sales reflected "both the prosperity and patriotism of that particular portion of the MSA area in which he lives."

Dad in RCAF uniform, with his father.

Bap was very influential in Dad's life, and in mine, too. Dad often spoke of him to me, both before and after his early demise from cancer in 1966, at age 64. Dad told me that he desperately wanted to join up for war service, but his father would have none of it, until Dad reached the age of 18.

Here are some comments of Gordon Bretelle, about Bap (who he called Uncle Buster):

> *"Uncle Buster was more involved in politics than any other members of the family, as I remember. He could get quite intense about issues. I seem to recall he was the most articulate of the Taylors at that time; a conservative politically. Of course I paid absolutely no attention to politics; all I can remember is that at times there were strong debates amongst Uncle Buster, Uncle Gordy and Old Man. What the debates were about I have no idea. I would have remembered if the issues had concerned peanut-butter cookies."*

I have devoted Chapter 4 of this book to the Forrester family; but I want to mention that the Forrester girls were about to loom large in Bap's life. Gwladys Forrester met and married Samuel Nicholson (of the Mount Lehman Nicholson pioneer family). Somehow Bap was introduced to Gwladys's sister Dorothy Forrester, and they married in 1921, at Bellingham, Washington. The Forrester girls' parents, James Grant Forrester and Elizabeth Douglas Forrester, bought a house and property in Mount Lehman about 1919 or 1920, thus becoming neighbours of the Taylor families.

Dorothy was a city girl, having been born in Edinburgh, Scotland, then moving with her family to Philadelphia, Pennsylvania for a few years, and then relocating to Vancouver, BC, where they lived in the Kitsilano district. I remember her telling me that she liked to attend ice hockey games with her father, at an arena in the West End of Vancouver, but that her mother was apprehensive that she would get hit by an errant puck (as there was no netting or glass around the playing surface of the rink). I wish I knew exactly how Granny met Bap, but it is one of those questions I never asked. Granny was a school teacher, having received her training at Vancouver Normal School, and, before she married Bap, she taught at Bradner School.

Our family was very close with Granny and Bap; during my years of growing up, they lived three houses south of us, on the corner of Burgess and Mount Lehman Road. Bap was a partner, with Uncle Jim and Dad, in the general store business called Taylors Farm Service. That business sold everything from animal feed, groceries, and hardware, and Bap ran the mechanic's shop which was a part of the Taylors Farm Service building at 5913 Mount Lehman Road.

In addition to his mechanical work, and his farming, (he continued to look after the family farm on Taylor Road until his death). Bap was interested in politics, being a staunch Conservative supporter. In 1954 he was the Provincial Conservative standard-bearer in the election, for our riding, although he was unsuccessful in being elected.

He launched the above campaign while already elected to Matsqui Municipal Council, serving as a Councillor from 1953 until his untimely death from cancer, in 1966. He was also a Justice of the Peace in Matsqui, however I do not know if that involved sitting in court, or whether it simply allowed him to notarize documents.

Here are some personal reminiscences of Bap. I was only 16 when he died, but I spent a lot of time with him during my youth. He was very active in Mount Lehman United Church for years; in fact, during lean years of the church I would say that he and Granny, amongst others, kept the church going when odds were against it. He taught me to light the wood and coal furnace at the church - that was my job on Sunday mornings.

L to R, Bap, Les Ayres M.L.A., Joe Merryfield.

1961 Matsqui Council Photo - Bap in front on left.

Bap was a mechanic at Taylors Farm Service, looking after many customers by providing maintenance to their vehicles. His shop was well stocked with tools, a car hoist, and welding and other equipment. I would work at the "store" after school and on weekends, and

Bap, as acting Reeve of Matsqui, officiating at the Bradner May Day festivities.

H.E. Buster Taylor's campaign poster for the 1954 Provincial General Election

witnessed first hand his expertise in his shop. Many times he would ask me to help him with jobs like bleeding brakes, and providing a second set of hands on particular jobs. I believe he instilled in me an interest in mechanics, which has continued to the present. He was quite a jokester at times; I remember one time, when he was lowering a car down on the hoist, he starting yelling "Gord, help me, my foot is caught under the hoist", so I ran over and flipped the hoist lever to raise it, and looked around to see if he was alright, only to see a big smile, and to realize his foot was fine, and he had played a joke at my expense.

I remember that Bap owned an old tugboat (I'm not sure where he got it), which he kept tied up in the river, at the bottom of Landing Road, which road was still passable by car right down to the river in those days. He kept the tug tied to a piling and he used it as a pleasure craft. I remember riding in it on the Fraser.

I also have pleasant memories of our whole extended family (our family, and Uncle Jim's) attending at my grandparents' house, on Burgess Road, for holidays and special occasions. I will never forget the Christmas when Bap bought Grant and I BB guns for Christmas, and that, because of inclement weather outside, we were each allowed to shoot the new guns in their kitchen, using the kitchen door as a target. (For some reason, Granny and Mum were not that impressed!)

I also remember accompanying my grandparents on trips over to the Taylor Road farm, where they would go to upkeep the property - sometimes we would have picnics there with them. Bap looked after that farm, in addition to his mechanic's duties, and his responsibilities on Matsqui Council. He had inherited the eastern 80 acres of the Taylor farms, after the deaths of Burton, Anna and John, whereas Uncle Gordy inherited the western 80 acres of the Taylor farms, after the deaths of Ed, Lizzie and Herb. Bap didn't have a lot of free time!

Bap and his father (Ed) fishing at the Fraser.

My grandparents owned a 1955 Chev 2-door sedan when I was a kid (I also know that prior to that car, Bap owned an Austin A40). Their favourite spot to go for holidays was Canim Lake, in the BC Cariboo, where they would venture for summer getaways.

Granny was a also a stalwart of the Mount Lehman community, especially the church. Both she and Bap regularly attended the church from their marriage in 1921. Granny was the church organist for many years and also served on the church board. I actually served on the church board with her at one point. She was also a volunteer librarian at Mount Lehman's Public Library, which was housed at various locations from about 1930 on. See Appendix 4, " History of Mount Lehman Public Library", written by Granny.

My grandparents started their married life in a house on Taylor Road. They lived in this house until Uncle Jim and Aunt Ellen married in 1944, and then they moved into the old farmhouse next door (at 30004 Taylor) until 1953, when they bought a house at the corner of Burgess and Mount Lehman Road. It is the Burgess address where they lived when I was a child.

Although as a kid I had taken piano lessons from Mrs. Ellen Stewart (who lived on Satchell Road), Granny decided to teach me to play church hymns on the old pump organ at our church, and then she decided I was ready (I wasn't so sure) to play at the church services on Sundays, which I did for several years.

Granny in the Mount Lehman Library

The family in front of the Burgess Road house, into which Granny and Bap moved
about 1950. Photo taken about 1980. L to R: Grant, me, Doug, Brian James
Kingman, Donna Kingman, Madeline (Grant's first wife), Karen, Auntie Ellen,
Suzanne, Granny, Dad, Ryan, Sharon, Mum, Rose and Uncle Jim.

I spent a lot of time with her, especially after she was widowed in 1966. She did not drive a car until Bap died, but at the age of 65, she vowed to learn! Then, she wanted to trade in their car (about a 62 Acadian, I believe), so I went with her to Riverside Chev-Olds in Mission, where she bought a Plymouth Duster 2-door sedan, a car which she owned until she stopped driving. She was never quite sure that the car would stay put when she parked somewhere, so she kept a 2x4 behind her seat, so she could place it behind a rear wheel when she stopped.

Granny relaxing at Mum and Dad's house.

I would help her around the house, with little fix-it projects, but she was very independent - I remember her telling me that her basement drain backed up in the middle of the night, (she was in her mid-80s then), so she had to make her way to the gully at the back of her house, and kind of crawl along the top of the gully to the end of the drain pipe, and using some kind of pole she found, she dislodged the blockage. Also, as she got older (she lived in her house until in her mid-90s), without telling my brother Grant or me, she dragged a stepladder from her outside shed, up her back stairs and into the kitchen, and promptly climbed it and fell and broke her arm - this was the beginning of her health downfall.

The house on Taylor Road in which Dad and Uncle Jim were raised -Granny is holding Uncle Jim in this photo.

Another activity shared between Granny (who was the sponsor/leader) and her grandchildren, including me, was membership in the Junior Orange Lodge, which conducted its meetings in the lodge room on the second storey of the Mount Lehman Orange Hall. My brother Grant and my cousins Donna and Janet also attended. It was very interesting to see the inner workings of the Lodge, and being taught the old favourite hymns and bible verses, as they were interspersed during the meetings. I considered this another important aspect of my education. The first verse of one of my favourites, sung at Lodge, is:

> *"The Maple Leaf Forever*
> *In days of yore,*
> *From Britain's shore*
> *Wolfe the dauntless hero came*
> *And planted firm Britannia's flag*
> *On Canada's fair domain.*
> *Here may it wave,*
> *Our boast, our pride*
> *And joined in love together,*
> *The thistle, shamrock, rose entwined,*
> *The Maple Leaf forever."*

Granny was so active, and so independent; it was a shame to see her have to leave her house; she spent her last few years, first with Uncle Jim, for a year or so, and latterly at Val Haven Rest Home in Mount Lehman. I found it difficult to visit her there, and see her health going downhill. She died in September, 1999, in her 99th year.

Among my notes, I found "A Tribute in Memory of Dorothy Taylor", written by Rev. Wayne Wattman, one of the ministers at our church, at the time of her passing, in 1999. I quote from it here:

"Of all the good folk who have 'pulled the oar' to make the Good Ship Mount Lehman United sail with confidence and strength over the many years, the name of Dorothy Forrester Taylor shall be recorded this past year and always as a loyal member of the crew of Jesus Christ. Her passing in 1999 closed

Granny, taken on our deck on Burgess Road.

a very notable page in the history of our congregation and she will be long remembered with pride and affection .... With her husband Buster in our congregation, serving on the official board, playing the old pump organ you now view in the sanctuary; and she was very instrumental in helping keep the church 'alive and well' when other voices thought it best to close the work. ... We salute the firm Christian faith she embraced and remember the stirring words of William Walsham, when today we think of her:

'For all the saints who from their labours rest,
Who Thee by faith before the world confessed
Thy Name, O Jesus, be forever blest, Hallelujah, Hallelujah!

Thou wast their rock, their Fortress, and their Might:
Thou Lord, their Captain in the well-fought fight;
Thou in the darkness drear their one true Light,
Hallelujah, Hallelujah! ' "

Katherine Mary Louise (Taylor) Bretelle

The next of Ed and Lizzie's children is Katherine Mary Louise, who was born on December 27, 1906, the same year that Ed and Lizzie moved to Mount Lehman. She was known as "Aunt Kitty" to Dad and us kids. Some of the information which follows is paraphrased from her obituary, which was written by her son, Gordon Bretelle, when she died in 2005. She began to take piano lessons at age 5, studying classical music. She was also very fond of jazz. I am not sure where she took piano lessons at a very young age, but I know she travelled to New Westminster later on for lessons. She would have travelled there from Mount Lehman station on board the Inter-Urban tram, which started service in about 1910.

She took piano lessons for many years, and received a certificate from the Royal Academy of Music in Canada. My previous notes tell that she played piano in a band with Bap, and travelled up and down the Fraser Valley to do so.

In 1928, she married Ted Bretelle, and the couple later moved to Washington State. Ted was a drummer, and they played in various clubs in the Olympia, Washington area.

Aunt Kitty at about 20 years of age.

Dad and his Aunt Kitty at the piano, 1987.

In 1948, Aunt Kitty moved to Union, Oregon, and began giving piano lessons to area students, as well as providing a music program for Keating, Oregon's one room school. She also played for many funerals and weddings throughout the area, and playing at weddings of former students was always a special occasion for her. (In 1971, she played for Sharon and my wedding.)

Aunt Kitty next to her brother Uncle Gordy's shack, with Gordy's dog Jeff.

Aunt Kitty's favourite pastime was fishing, and at the slightest suggestion, she had her lunch and fishing gear packed and was ready to head for a stream or lake. Aunt Kitty died in 2005, survived by her son Gordon of Union, Oregon, two grandchildren, Selena and Bret, and nieces and nephews.

Our family always had good times with Aunt Kitty when she visited from Oregon. We would go fishing down to the Fraser, or we would take her to our place at Loon Lake in the Cariboo. And we invariably ended up around the piano, listening to her play all the tunes that she had been playing for years. Such a wonderful woman!

The front page of the program for one of Aunt Kitty's recitals, 1952.

Dad and Aunt Kitty after a good day's fishing at our lot at Loon Lake.

Gordon William Frederick Taylor

Last, but not least, I write about Gordon William Frederick Taylor, (Uncle Gordy), the youngest child of Ed and Lizzy, who was born on June 15, 1908. He was an amazingly clever individual! I regret only knowing him for ten years, as he was tragically killed as a pedestrian, by a hit-and-run driver, in 1959, the identity of which driver has never been found.

Uncle Gordy at about 5 years of age.

While I would regularly visit him, with Dad, much of the narrative in this story about him has been told to me by others.

Uncle Gordy lived in his parents' house from the time the house was built, until the 1950s. He too attended Mount Lehman School. I remember that when I attended Mount Lehman School in the 1950s, I saw Uncle Gordy's initials carved into the windowsill in what was then the teachers' staffroom. He was raised as a farm kid, of course, and would have assisted his family, as well as Herb and John. It seems, from hearing family stories, that Ed, Bap and Gordy not only farmed their own farm, but as Herb and John got older, they also did chores for them, including milking cows. But the talents of Uncle Gordy extended far beyond normal farm work. Dad had told me many stories about Uncle Gordy. It is obvious to me that Dad held Uncle Gordy in the highest regard. This esteem and regard is also echoed in Gordon Bretelle's stories from his time in Mount Lehman from 1936-1944. Here are some of his recollections:

"*Uncle Gordy demonstrated the most interest in me of any on the farm. When the work of the day was done; when there was machinery to service or repair; or when there was something to invent and construct, he would invite me to 'help' or to just watch. He was an amazing person. Truly a renaissance man compared to any of his peers. Before electricity came to the farm in about 1946, Gordy had electricity in his shop by way of an old Model T Ford engine, which was securely mounted on two large pieces of timber, and drove a large dynamo which he had acquired from someone. The Model T engine also powered a wood lathe in the shop through a belt drive devised by Gordy. Of course he built the lathe himself. I'm not too certain of this, but I believe*

Uncle Gordy

he had a jigsaw as well. [author's note: I remember this jigsaw well - when I first saw it, it was located at the store building on Mount Lehman Road, and I used it when I was a kid to make house name signs or number signs for our relatives - I charged 15 cents per letter or number. I remember I made one for Granny and Bap]."

"*In Gordy's shop, there was a pottery wheel he made from a flywheel salvaged from either a piece of farm machinery, or an old truck engine. Inertia was provided to the flywheel by a pivoted beam attached to a substantial rod, welded or bolted to the upper face of the wheel. By applying force to the wooden beam in a rhythmic manner with his foot, rotation would be given to the potter's wheel above through a steel bar about three feet in length. Clay was found somewhere on the property nearby, and through all this self-conceived process, Gordy fashioned many artful pieces of pottery, one of which was given to my mother and is now in my possession. This small vessel is particularly meaningful to me since, on the bottom, written in Gordy's neat lettering, with a fine scribe, reads 'June 24.1937' and his stylized initials, 'GT'."*

"About the time that Gordy was making this vessel for my mother, Jimmy, Doug and I would have been sprawled out on the ground watching Uncle Gordy place this piece of pottery, and others, in a crude oven he had fashioned in the mound of tailings from the water well, which had been dug at a distance of about forty feet down the slope south of the kitchen porch of the old house where we lived! Firing his pottery was an event that occurred maybe four times during the summer. And it was much more than just firing his pottery. It was something we boys anticipated greatly. It would be the time of watching Gordy carefully lay the wood which would provide the coals for the process. This would be done with the final reddish glow of the sunset lighting the sky. It probably took an hour or more for the right amount of coals to be formed. With the open end of the 'oven' giving heat and some light, we would lay on our backs looking up into a now blackening sky as Gordy would point out to us many of the constellations, how they moved, the planets, the North Star. He would try to simply give us a bit of the theory of the creation of all we could see in the sky. The way in which he explained these things ensured our rapt attention."

"After the firing process was done, we would each place a large potato, which we brought with us, into the dwindling coals, turning them until they were charred all around and then remove them to cool a bit. We'd cut them open and eat the soft, well-baked interior, with spoons. There

Here is Uncle Gordy in his Model T Ford - looks like the Mission Bridge in the background.

have never been nights more profound to me than these."

"Gordy was an inventor. He was an electrician; a mechanical engineer; a radio technician; an animal trainer; a carpenter; a teacher, and a patriot. He was the closest thing to a positive role model I ever had during all of my childhood. [author's note: maybe this was why Aunt Kitty sent her son to Mount Lehman for the summers?] ...I remember when he devised a very effective electric fence for the large pasture bordering the old house. He constructed it using a six volt car battery, a Model T coil, an interruptor device using automobile ignition distributor points and a long piece of flat copper metal and some gears from an old alarm clock! He isolated one of the middle wires of the barbed wire fence that encircled the pasture, by using small patches of rubber cut from an automobile tire, which he attached to each fencepost, allowing current to flow completely around the pasture. I can personally attest to the effectiveness of this system .....!"

"*Gordy constructed an exceptional radio from plans he found in a copy of Popular Mechanics. He acquired the parts from a supply house mentioned in the magazine article. The radio brought in stations from all over Western Canada and the United States, especially at night. Not only that, but it received short wave signals from many different places. He then built a beautiful shelf cabinet for the radio; and later an impressive floor console. This, incidentally, was the radio through which we heard news of the war in Europe, the Battle of Britain, and the attack on Pearl Harbour. [author's note: this radio and stereo system was first seen by me in the mid-1950s in Uncle Gordy's cabin; I remember listening to Hank Snow on the record player built into this system].*"

"*Uncle Gordy was also good with animals. I'm not sure how many dogs he had. Only two are in my memories. They were both Collies, and were both named 'Jeff'. The first Jeff was a remarkable dog. The second was equally smart and well trained. Jeff #1 was a little closer to my heart in that he was my companion during my first couple of summers when my lonely times were most frequent and intense. I particularly have held the memory of sitting on the lawn at the northeast corner of the house, feeling so very homesick for my parents and the land I knew; and Jeff coming to sit next to me as I stared at the mountains to the north, far away across the valley. I'd put my arm around him and he would seem to lean into me. He'd feel nice and warm. Then I would frequently take the harmonica someone had given me out of my pocket and start to blow into it, whereupon Jeff would point his nose at the sky and make the most mournful sounds. It seemed so fitting! He'd play ball with me and we'd chase one another ... the best times were when Uncle Gordy would come in from milking or work in the fields. Jeff would do almost anything Gordy asked him to do. Gordy would tell him to climb the apple tree near the back porch, and the dog would do just that! Once on a limb maybe eight feet off the ground, Gordy would put out his arms, forming a cradle, and tell Jeff to 'jump'. Jeff would follow that command without hesitation! Gordy wouldn't catch him, but would slow his flight through the air enough that the dog would touch the ground unhurt. Once, when Mum and Dad had come to pick me up and take me home at the end of the summer, Gordy got Jeff to jump out of Gordy's second story bedroom window, with the same results! I think my Mum almost fainted! Another of Jeff's amazing feats was climbing the same vertical ladder I used to gain access to the grain loft in the barn. The dog was truly amazing and fearless. I don't remember him ever getting hurt. Jeff #2 was not quite as amazing as #1, but just as affection-ate. I was equally saddened when I heard of the deaths of both dogs, both of old age. [author's note; I remember Dad telling me that when Uncle Gordy was killed, in 1959, his dog Jeff started barking, and would not stop- it was as if he knew his master had died.]"*

"Uncle Gordy had a shop near his father's house. Whenever anyone; neighbours, friends or family would visit his shop, he would give them a light blue 4x5" card and ask them to write something and autograph the card. He would then tack the card on the south wall of the shop, just inside the entrance door. These cards accumulated over a few years to the point where Gordy had to stop the tradition. I'd give a lot to know where

those cards went; they covered most of the years of WWII, and some of the writers didn't survive war service . One in particular whom I remember was a school friend of Gordy's or Buster's ... or perhaps the son or nephew of a friend of Old Man's... I just can't remember. Anyhow, he was a very impressive man to me; dark and handsome in his RCAF uniform. He was a Hawker Hurricane fighter pilot on his last leave before going overseas. Being an airplane nut since the age of three, I was absolutely enthralled by tales of learning to fly and fight in the sky, which he told to me as I peppered him with questions. On his card, before he left, he wrote 'to Big and Little Gordon, when the Great Scorer comes; to mark against your name, he'll mark not how you won or lost, but how you played the game.' I was told the following year that he was killed in a dogfight over Antwerp, after downing three Me-109 fighters himself. I remember that Gordy was visibly saddened for several days after getting the news."

"The most mystifying invention Gordy gave to the government during WWII was one which Doug and I discussed several times during our adult lives. As I recall, it involved a device which would render German navy mine-sweeping efforts practically useless. The device would allow a cable, towed between two mine-sweeping vessels travelling parallel courses, to pass through the tethering cables used to keep the mines just below the water's surface, instead of cutting

the tethering cables, allowing the mines to float to the surface where they could be harmlessly exploded with rifle fire! I don't know about Doug; but trying to imagine the workings of this device caused me many sleepless nights before I finally gave up the quest."

Of course, I am not sure whether Uncle Gordy's inventions were actually employed during the war effort, but this shows the inventiveness of the mind of Uncle Gordy. I also remember Dad telling me that Uncle Gordy invented the method of opening a band-aid with a string inserted in it - long before Band-Aid came up with the idea commercially. Unfortunately, Uncle Gordy didn't patent any of his inventions!

Back to Gordon Bretelle's notes again.

"Another of my favourite childhood relatives was my cousin Doug. We were close in age (he being born in 1924, I in 1929). And also because Doug was an adventurer, and that certainly appealed to my nature. We both LOVED airplanes. Real or models. Doug and I became pals in the first summer or two of my visits to Mount Lehman. We did many things together and hatched many adventurous projects."

"Doug and I constructed bows and arrows with materials collected from around the farm. The arrows were fashioned from slices of cedar shakes, sanded round, with pheasant feathers and .22 calibre shell casings at each end. My arrows flew pretty well, though inconsistently. Doug's bows and arrows were truly impressive. He could consistently shoot his arrows all the way across the pasture from the front lawn of the house! Mine were usually good for perhaps fifty yards. Nevertheless, this was real fun. ... Next were slings like David used against Goliath. Our first attempts were less than impressive, due mainly to materials used in construction: binder twine and thin bicycle inner

tubes. We also struggled with technique. Gordy came in on this project as both advisor and materials sub-contractor. Leather pockets and sturdy leather thongs vastly improved the speed and range of our stones; and later, a small supply of one inch ball bearings greatly improved both our accuracy and lethality. This became evident one evening after supper when we went out back to the barn where we had made about a three foot circle, on the barn wall, with chalk. From about fifty feet out, Doug wound up vigorously and released his shot; he missed the circle by about a foot, but put a jagged eight or ten inch hole in one of the 1x12 planks of the barn wall. I'll never forget the expression on his face as we looked at each other in unexpected amazement! It was a mixture of pride and fear. We ran around the entrance and into the darkening barn. You simply couldn't miss seeing that hole! OK. Put the piece back in place and no one will notice!! As we got to the hole we discovered there was not one piece, but many pieces ...shards, like broken glass. We hurried to Gordy's shop to confess and seek a solution to the problem. As he had done more than once, Gordy saved our bacon. After viewing the damage, he returned to the shop, cut two rectangular pieces of metal, grabbed a handful of finishing nails, a hammer, a small can of flat grey implement paint, and a brush, and made inside and outside patches which were almost invisible unless you got very close to them. With the vertical strokes of the brush, he even made a very close approximation of the grain pattern of the board."

"Doug and I really got to be pals when we started building model airplanes together. At about age 9, I had become obsessed with building model airplanes- both non-flying scale models

and flying models. Hand gliders were also intriguing. I would arrive at the farm with two or three kits ready to be assembled. Doug would join me in translating the printed plans into flying hardware. It was often tedious work, requiring lots of patience, and he was largely responsible for my developing that trait. First flights were always charged with emotion. I can vividly remember Doug's body-english contortions whenever one of the planes appeared to be headed for certain disaster into a tree or fence. It wasn't long before I too adopted this manner of imparting guidance to the craft, which might be fifty feet away. A couple of years later, Gordy confided in us how much laughter we created in the living room as family members watched this awkward ballet!"

"One of the most enjoyable gliders I brought to the farm was one which had spring loaded folding wings which could be launched to fairly great heights with a heavy rubber band. As the glider would reach the top of this vertical trajectory and slowed, the wings would snap out and it would soar about for many seconds; often minutes. What really made this glider so enjoyable was watching the barn swallows mistake it for a marauding hawk, and swoop at it from all angles, trying to scare it away. Also, Doug designed a rubber-powered pusher propeller flying wing, which flew remarkably well. This was a good many years before any of the world's aircraft designers found it feasable to do the same."

"Up until 1939 or 1940, I seem to recall that Uncle Gordy, Old Man and I would walk together down to Uncle John's barn, morning and evening, to milk. On the way, we would herd along any cows which had wandered up by the dam, or points

along the way. If it was a Friday night, Jimmy and Doug would join us, because Friday nights were the nights when they would sleep over. This was a sort of tradition, I believe."

The British Government's response to Uncle Gordy's letters, suggesting a new type of anti-aircraft shell, and a new mine-sweeping technique.

"The war in Europe was in full swing; and rationing had come to Canada. I remember that Gabby had to apply for an extra ration book for me, to allow for the extra foods which I would consume. This would continue for the duration. Sugar was one of the rationed foods. This posed a real problem for Gordy one summer. He had decided that since he had acquired some bottles somewhere, he'd put them to use by making a batch of home brewed beer. Some of the ingredients needed to be improvised - sugar being the most important. After a little thought, Gordy figured that barn molasses might do the trick in place of sugar. The concoctions, mixed and fermented in a large crock, seemingly completed, he implemented the bottling process one Friday evening. Using a hand capping device, he bottled maybe twenty bottles. We boys were not allowed in his shop while this procedure was done. Later that night, after Gabby had laid the law down to us about giggling and laughing at many of Gordy's jokes (we all slept in Gordy's bedroom, where there were two huge beds), silence fell over the house. ... around midnight, Jimmy woke Gordy up (thereby waking Doug and me) and said he heard a 'popping sound and

glass breaking'. Gordy was up in an instant and was pulling on his overalls and putting on his shoes as he went down the stairs yelling at us in a hushed voice to stay in our room. We heard more popping and broken glass for a few more minutes, then silence. Gordy came back to bed after a while and nothing more was said until we had breakfast the following morning, and prepared to go down for milking. Old Man said he heard the noise and asked Gordy about it. We couldn't help but bust out laughing every few steps down to the barn, as we imagined the scene of Gordy throwing an old piece of canvass over the bottles to protect himself from flying glass and spraying beer; and in the pitch blackness, feeling for unexploded bottles with an opener in his hand, trying to get the caps off before impending disaster! Gabby tried her best not to show the smile curling at the corners of her mouth."

As noted above, Uncle Gordy lived in his parents' house until sometime in the 1950s. From about 1948, when Herb died, he took over Herb's farm and operated it until about mid-1950s, when he rented his old family home, along with Herb's barn and entire farm, to the Andringa family. (My cousin Donna told me that Ed's barn had collapsed in the 1980s.) It was at this time that Gordy constructed the cabin in front of which you see Aunt Kitty standing, with Gordy's dog.

My cousins Donna and Janet tell me that Uncle Gordy worked in logging camps from about 1943-1948, (they tell me he may have also worked there prior to his father's death in 1943) in the coastal areas of British Columbia. He would have had the equivalent of a millright's position at those mills. So adept was he at keeping the mill equipment operating and in good condition that it is said that if he wasn't present at the millsite, the mill at times shut down; they missed his expertise so much!

GORDON W.F. TAYLOR

Uncle Gordy behind a log truck, during his days as a millwright.

I'll end this Chapter with an anecdote about Uncle Gordy, epitomizing his sense of humour. Apparently the Nicholson family of Mount Lehman installed electricity to power its house and farm, about 1921. A day or so after the electric lights and power were being enjoyed by the Danny Nicholson family at dinnertime, Uncle Gordy and Sam Nicholson decided to have a little fun. While the meal was taking place, Sam ignited a stick of dynamite, and threw it in the yard of the house, making a huge blast, and digging a crater in the yard; at the same time, on cue, Uncle Gordy went down to the basement of the house and flipped off the main electrical breaker, plunging the entire house into darkness. So the Nicholson family thought that some major hydro-electrical disaster had befallen them! Then, of course, Uncle Gordy and Sam made haste to get out of there! I don't know how long it took for the Nicholsons to figure out what had actually happened, but I can tell you that the people of Mount Lehman knew and told this story for years afterward!

The next Chapter details Granny's Forrester family, and how they got to Mount Lehman.

Chapter 4

THE FORRESTER FAMILY AND MOUNT LEHMAN

The story of Dad and the Taylor family would not be complete without mentioning the Forresters, Granny Taylor's family, who moved to Mount Lehman in about 1919, or so. First, some background, starting with the patriarch, James Grant Forrester, Granny's father, and continuing with her mother, Elizabeth Douglas Forrester.

James Grant Forrester and Elizabeth Douglas ("Flossie") (Roulston) Forrester

Mr. Forrester was born in 1866, in Edinburgh, Scotland. He was the youngest of five children. Granny told me that the Forrester family originally lived in the village of Corstorphine, Scotland, which had been the ancestral home of the Forresters for hundreds of years. James's father was William Forrester, and his mother was Alice (Fordie) Forrester. They were married on 29 February, 1856, at Edinburgh. His father, William Forrester, died in 1878, and is buried at Old Dalry Cemetery, Edinburgh. While James lived in Edinburgh, his brother John owned a newsagent and bookstore business in Londonderry, Northern Ireland, and when James was visiting his

brother John in Londonderry on one occasion, he met his future
wife, Elizabeth Douglas Roulston, my great-grandmother, whom
he called "Flossie". James and his wife Elizabeth were married on
August 17, 1892, at Castlerock, Northern Ireland

James had obtained a Master of Arts degree (M.A.) from the
University of Edinburgh. He then apprenticed (as they called it
then) to a firm of solicitors in Edinburgh- Balfour and Company,
from 1885, (Note: since James was not yet 21 years old, his mother,
Alice (Fordie) Forrester, was required to be a party to the agreement
by which James apprenticed to Balfour and Company (although she
died the next year, on 29 May, 1886)- Granny gave me a copy of this
apprenticeship document, and James was called to the Scottish Bar
in 1896, to be what was called a "Law Agent", the equivalent of what
we call in Canada a solicitor. He practised law with that firm until
1904; his practise consisted of the usual solicitor's practise, which
included representing a client named Cresswell Ranche and Cattle
Co. Ltd, which had interests both in Britain and in the U.S.A. A
note I found amongst James's papers says that this company owned
180,000 acres outright (on the Texas Panhandle), and pastured over
1,200,000 acres of land.

The family lived at 167 Morningside Road, in Edinburgh. Granny
told me that her mother sang in the same church choir as James.
James's family was Congregationalist, whereas his wife's family was
Presbyterian. I found a letter dated 18 May, 1904, from Morningside
Congregational Church, containing the following:

"*My dear Forrester,*

*At a meeting of the Church held tonight, reference was made
to the departure to America of you and Mrs. Forrester, and
to the services which you had rendered to the Church, and I*

was instructed to forward to you the following copy of a resolution passed at the Meeting: 'That this Meeting of Members of Morningside Congregational church, Edinburgh, desires to express its warm appreciation of the services of Mr. James G. Forrester, as Secretary to the Managers, as a member of the Choir, and in other offices, for many years: wishes him, Mrs. Forrester, and family, God speed on their journey to the United States, and trusts they may all have a happy settlement in their new home'... Expression was also given to our regret at the loss sustained by us through your departure from Edinburgh... Yours very sincerely, ...Acting Secretary."

In 1904, James was offered a job in Texas with his client Cresswell, and so he decided to move to the U.S., with his family, to take the job opportunity. I have copies of some of the letters of recommendation given to him by clients and colleagues at the Balfour firm, at the time he left Scotland. Excerpts from these follow:

From James's employer, Leslie Melville Balfour:

"... you came to this office as an apprentice to my original Firm of Messrs. J. & J. H. Balfour in 1885 and since 1896 have acted as principal Clerk with us much to our advantage and to our entire satisfaction. Your experience with us has been in all the branches of our business and in all of these your method of work and capabilities for it have been of the highest order. ... You have had entire control of our many cash transactions and kept our Accounts and Books in a manner which left nothing to be desired. You have also had charge of the Books and Registers kept by me as Agent in this city for the Australian Deposit and Mortgage Bank Ltd., Melbourne. For the satisfaction of those

who wish to know I may add that your habits and conduct are above reproach. We wish you every success in your new life."

From John D. Hope, Esq., M.P. for West Fifeshire, Scotland:

"I became acquainted with Mr. James G. Forrester in connection with The Cresswell Ranche and Cattle Co. Ltd., of which I was at one time Secretary, and afterwards a Director, ... I had ample opportunities of forming an opinion on Mr. Forrester's character and abilities. ...he looked after the financial arrangements involving this large corporation, which were of a very complicated nature, constantly involving the consideration of points of a semi-legal nature, and in dealing with these, Mr. Forrester's legal training was of invaluable service to the Company and saved it considerable sums ...Mr. Forrester gained the confidence and respect of the Board and his having to attend to many other duties showed that he was methodical and a thoroughly capable man. ... I have every confidence in recommending him to anyone desiring a capable, steady and obliging servant. Most gladly will I hear of his success."

From Rev. John Gillespie, LLD, Ex-Moderator of Established Church of Scotland:

"...Mr. Forrester has always borne a high character as a man of honour and integrity and I feel sure he would give satisfaction in any situation where business capacity and experience as well as reliability are required."

From Henry Brown, Esq., Manager Century Insurance Co., Ltd. Edinburgh:

"I am very much interested to learn that you are about to make your home in the United States of America, and I do not need to say, I think, how sincerely I hope and believe that if as one generally understands, intelligence, energy and ability count for anything in America, you will have a successful future there."

A copy of the first page of the document filed in the Scottish Court, to admit James Grant Forrester as a "law agent" (lawyer) in Scotland.

James left for America approximately three months before the rest of his family, in order to find accommodation and get organized in his new job. But on the ship over to the U.S., he met a man named Rattray, (according to Granny), who convinced him to take a job with the Girard Trust Company of Philadelphia, rather than take the job with Cresswell. It must have been interesting for his wife to receive this news! So his vocation as a lawyer ended in Scotland; he never practised law again- Granny told me that the practise of law in the U.S. did not seem to appeal to him. Instead he took the job with Girard Trust, where he worked for over two years, until 1906.

My great-grandmother, Elizabeth Forrester, (whom we great-grandchildren called "Gaby", (not to be confused with Gabby (Lizzie) Taylor, mentioned in previous chapters, was born in Londonderry, Northern Ireland, in 1870 . Her father was George Roulston, who was a ship's captain on a sailing ship, and who only returned home every 4 months or so

A document found in Dad's papers, showing that by 1862, Gaby Forrester's father, George Roulston, had a Certificate of Competency in the UK Merchant Service. By the time of his death, in Galveston, Texas, he had attained the position of Master or Captain.

Unfortunately, he died as a result of asphyxiation on board the ship, of which he was the Master (caused by coal fumes) while docked in Galveston, Texas, in 1884, and he is buried in a Masonic cemetery there. Gaby's mother, Mary Jane Douglass, died giving birth to a son, David (who also died at birth), and Gaby and her brothers were raised by their grandmother. Her brothers, Robert and George, at some point, moved to Louisville, Kentucky and married women who were sisters, in about 1904. Gaby kept in touch with her brothers over the years, and when she lived in British Columbia, Granny said she travelled to Kentucky to visit them on at least one occasion.

Much of the content of Gaby's family history, noted in this chapter, was told to me by Granny Taylor when I interviewed her in the 1980s. When the family decided to move to America in 1904, Gaby, Granny, her sister Gwladys, and Elizabeth (James's sister) temporarily went to Ireland, and lived with Aunt Lizzie Wray, a widow (and Granny's aunt), who lived at Castlerock, Northern Ireland (near Londonderry). Aunt Lizzy had a farm there. Even though she was only three years old, Granny remembered that while staying there, a goat would sometimes run through the house. She also recalled riding in an Irish "Jonting car", a horse drawn cart with seats facing sideways. In 2014, during a visit to Ireland, Sharon and I went to Castlerock; we also went to the cemetery there, looking for the graves of any members of the Wray or Roulston clans.

As to the trip to the U.S., Granny said she recalled James's brother John (the newsagent in Londonderry) carrying her onto the ship "Astoria", an Anchor Line ship. I found the manifest regarding the family's trip, which indicates that the ship left from Londonderry, and its destination was New York. Granny said she remembered being checked over by a doctor at the time of boarding. She said the whole family got sea-sick during the three-week voyage.

Granny related the following to me about living in the Philadelphia area. It seems that they lived in both Bryn Mawr, Pennsylvania, and Philadelphia, during their years in Pennsylvania. She told me she attended Ardmore Public School, near where the Autocar company had a plant. She said that prior to attending Ardmore, she attended a French private school in Bryn Mawr, but she didn't like it, so transferred to Ardmore. She said she played U.S. football in Bryn Mawr, with the boys, because there were no girls living on her street to play with. Granny's sister Gwladys, born in 1894, attended Bryn Mawr Public School, then Ardmore High School. Granny said that they walked to school, but sometimes they would get a lift from a man with a 1908 Ford car, with a bulb-style horn. I have a post-card, addressed to Granny, dated 1906, with the address 2341 S. 61st

Street, Philadelphia. I also have a post-card, addressed to Granny's sister Gwladys, addressed to 13 Barret Ave., Bryn Mawr, Pennsylvania.

This is my great-grandmother, Elizabeth (Flossie) Forrester, nee, Roulston, whom we called "Gaby".

Apparently while working at Girard Trust, among other clients, James handled the accounts of Bryn Mawr College, a prestigious women's school. Granny told me that while at Girard Trust, the principal of Bryn Mawr, a Miss Thomas, indicated to her father that the College needed a comptroller. James applied for, and got the job. She said Bryn Mawr was 14 miles out of Philadelphia, and that her father commuted to work on the Pennsylvania Railroad. James worked at Bryn Mawr College from 1906 to 1914.

Granny told me that when she was 13, her parents decided to move to Vancouver, B.C. Before they moved to Vancouver, though, Granny said they lived "temporarily" in Toronto, and stayed with a Mrs. Graver. Apparently they had known the Graver family for some time, as they for a number of years rented a cabin, on Head Lake in Ontario, from Mrs. Graver's brother. (I assume they travelled to Ontario each year from Philadelphia to stay in the cabin on the lake- Granny said they stayed there for a month each year.)

A youthful photo of James Grant Forrester during his law career in Edinburgh.

James and Elizabeth
(Flossie) Forrester.

Gwadys, James, Flossie
and Dorothy.

Granny said her mother and father talked a lot about the move to Vancouver; she said she didn't know how her father lined up the job in Vancouver, but it was located in the Credit Foncier Building, at 850 West Hastings Street. He may also been employed by the Standard Trust Company, as I found a post card, dated 1914, addressed to Jas. G. Forrester, Esq., "Manager, The Standard Trust Coy, Vancouver Block, Granville Street, Vancouver, BC." Dad told me that, at some point, James was with the Canadian Home Investment Company, and he travelled throughout British Columbia, indicating that the company had investments throughout the Province, which James managed or administered.

Granny and her father in the garden, Vancouver.

From L to R - Gaby, Uncle Jim, Bap, Uncle George
(Gaby's brother from Louisville, Kentucky), Granny.

Granny said they left Ontario by boat, via Fort William and Lakes Huron and Superior; they then travelled from Winnipeg to Vancouver by the Canadian Pacific Railroad, which took three days. In Vancouver, her parents rented a furnished house in the West End, as their furniture took several months to arrive. Later they moved to a rented house on 6th Ave., and still later, to a bigger rented house on Cornwall Street in Kitsilano. Granny attended "Normal School" in Vancouver, attaining her teaching certificate. Later, when the family moved to Mount Lehman, she taught at Bradner School. Granny's sister, Gwladys, wrote her entrance exam in Vancouver, for the University of Toronto, was accepted, and attended university there for four years, attaining a Bachelor of Arts. When she returned to B.C., she got a teaching job at Mount Lehman Elementary, boarding with the McCallums, just east of Mount Lehman United Church. Mount Lehman School was then a "Superior School", with Grades 1-11 - Gwladys was the principal, and taught Grades 8, 9, 10 and 11. It was apparently Gwladys who interested James and Elizabeth in buying property in Mount Lehman.

The family had lived in Vancouver for about five years before buying property in Mount Lehman, after which James "semi-retired", according to Granny. I have James and Elizabeth's income tax and accounting records, which indicate that, while James may have been semi-retired in Mount Lehman, he was still a salaried employee of The Canadian Home Investment Company, and the Alpha Mortgage and Investment Corporation. He also earned remuneration from the Coquitlam Terminal Company.

I spent some time going over the various bookkeeping and other records, of James and Elizabeth, and I found some interesting information about their purchase of property in Mount Lehman. They first purchased a 4.3 acre parcel of property, at 6134 Mount Lehman

Road, in 1919, for the sum of $350; the address shown for the Forresters, at the time of purchase, was 2455 Cornwall Street, Vancouver. After its purchase, this property was registered to Elizabeth Douglass Forrester. The vendor of this property was

L to R - Uncle Jim, Gaby, Mary-Elisabeth (Gwladys' daughter), Dad.

William Isaac Merryfield, of the pioneer Mount Lehman Merryfield family. This property was eventually given to the Forresters's daughter, Gwadys, who married Samuel Nicholson, of the Mount Lehman pioneer Nicholson family, and the house is still occupied as the home of Gwadys's and Sam's daughter, Mary-Elisabeth (Nicholson, Stadnyk) Iverson. Mary-Elisabeth also had a daughter, Nancy Stadnyk, but unfortunately she died at age 17, of leukemia.

I also found records indicating that James Grant Forrester, in 1920, purchased the house and 4.7 acres, located at 6184 Mount Lehman Road, (the next door parcel to 6134), for the sum of $3,300, from the Israel family. Then it seems that they spent some $1,800 in repairs and renovations on the house. I am not sure exactly when they moved to Mount Lehman; that is, whether they rented the house prior to the purchase, or did they not move to Mount Lehman until 1920? James commuted to work, probably several days per week (his office being in downtown Vancouver)- he would travel there by way of the Inter-Urban Railway, established in 1910, and which had a station in Mount Lehman. James spent approximately 10 years in Mount Lehman, until his death in 1929. My great-grandmother,

Gaby, lived in Mount Lehman for about 40 years, until her death in 1957.

Mr. Forrester was an astute investor, owning a portfolio of bonds and stocks, mortgages and loans, from which the family derived a comfortable income. However, James died on June 21, 1929, at the age of 64. Furthermore, as everyone knows, the stock market crash occurred on October 29, 1929. So poor great-grandmother Gaby had not only to contend with the death of her husband, but also the major stress of the devaluation of the family assets, which had to produce income for her for another almost 30 years, until her death in 1957. She was far from being a wealthy widow!

After the death of James, in 1929, Gaby lived alone in the 6184 Mount Lehman Road house, until Mum and Dad got married, in 1947, at which time she invited my mother and father to move into the upstairs of her house; she continued to live on the main floor. When I was born, in 1949, our family planned to move into a small cottage next door to Gaby's house - in fact, one of the two bedrooms in that cottage was wall-papered in cute little bunnies and things, in preparation for me to move in! That never happened, as Gaby decided that it was more suitable for her to move into the cottage, and for Mum and Dad to take over her big house. This is what occurred, and this is the house in which I and my brothers and sister were raised. Gaby lived next door in the cottage. It was such a privilege for me to know her from my birth in 1949, until her death, in 1957, at age 87. From my birth, Gaby called me her little "lambsy loozy", and spoiled me rotten.

From perusing the records of Mount Lehman United Church, it is evident that Gaby, and her two daughters, Gwladys and Granny, were very active in all aspects of Mount Lehman church life. I know Gaby also volunteered in the Mount Lehman library. An example of

Gaby's contribution to the church is exemplified in the inscription in the front of her hymn-book, given to her when she was in her late 70s, and which was given to me when Granny taught me piano and organ lessons, in the 1960s:

> *"Presented by Mt Lehman United Church*
> *To Mrs E. Forrester*
> *In appreciation of a life of*
> *Sunday school service*
> *(And the fact that, while enjoying a well earned retirement,*
> *She saw the need and returned to the work.)*
> *May 7, 1947.*
> *A. Sallis, Minister.*
>
> *Go, labour on: spend and be spent;*
> *Thy joy to do the Father's will;*
> *It is the way the Master went;*
> *Should not the servant tread it still?"*

A concluding story involving Gaby is that, in 1934, after her husband's death, she bought a building lot at 15240 Victoria Ave., White Rock, BC. In the Forresters's bookkeeping records, I note that Gaby paid $205.00 for the lot in 1934, and it cost her about $700.00 to build a cabin on it , as her son-in-law, Sam Nicholson, constructed it. She retained the property for the enjoyment of the family, and then she sold the lot, in 1942, for $1,000.00. I looked up this lot on the BC Assessment website. With a house built in 1992, it is currently assessed at $2,247,000.00! I wish we had it now! Dad told me many stories about spending summers in that cottage, with Gaby, Granny and Bap, Dad's brother Jim, and other family members. He said he also played golf on the White Rock beach, which was about 50 metres from this lot.

Chapter 5

DAD GROWING UP IN MOUNT LEHMAN

In the first four chapters of this book, I outlined how Dad's ancestors emigrated from England to North America, and spent about 120 years in what was to become the United States, and how they left (read this to mean "got kicked out") the US after the Revolutionary War, moving to Nova Scotia. I explained that Burton's branch of the Taylor family spent roughly 100 years in Nova Scotia, before Dad's great-grandmother availed herself of the offer of taking over the Bangs property in Mount Lehman. I also detailed the family's years in New Westminster, while they readied the Mount Lehman property for farming, by basically carving farms out of the forest. Then I detailed the establishment of the farms of John, Herb and Ed Taylor, and how they successfully farmed the property, from about 1893 until each of them retired from farming and their farms were taken over by Dad's Uncle Gordy and his brother, Dad's father Buster. Finally, I told the story of how Granny's parents, the Forresters, had moved to Mount Lehman about 1919.

When Dad was born in 1924, his parents lived on Taylor Road, in the house in which they had lived since they married in 1921. Dad's grandfather Ed had only lived in Mount Lehman for about

20 years when Dad was born. John and Herb independently farmed their parcels of land, with assistance from all family members - see the previous chapters providing the details. So when Dad (and his brother Jim,) were growing up, he had the good fortune of having all the family members I have previously mentioned, living in close proximity; - for example,

- his grandparents, Ed and Lizzy, who were in their 50s;
- his greatgrandmother, Anna, in her 80s;
- his great uncles, John and Herb, in their 50s;
- his uncle Gordy, still in his teens;
- his aunt Kitty, still in her teens;
- his brother Jim, age 2;
- his other grandparents, the Forresters, who were in their late 50s.

Dad and his brother were lucky to live with the entire Taylor clan (except, of course, Burton, who died in 1911) in Mount Lehman. What a privilege! They were all farmers, living an idyllic lifestyle, in days when they were no better, or worse off, financially, than their neighbours. The notes of Gordon Bretelle (Aunt Kitty's son, who was born in 1929,) which I have interspersed with family history, show the close relationships of all the family who resided on the Taylor lands. I am deeply indebted to Gordon Bretelle for these notes, as they tell the Taylors' stories in a first-hand manner.

According to an article about Dad's father, Buster, written by Dad's brother Jim in the 1993 publication, "The Place Between, Aldergrove and Communities" he says that, other than growing up on the farm, their father worked off the farm for a few years, before settling back into farm life:

"Buster got his education in Mt. Lehman School which had grades from one to eleven. He first worked at Cook's Mill, just south of the farm. After that, he drove a truck for the Provincial Highway Department and for Matsqui Municipality. About 1936, Buster and his brother Gordon were running the farm."

Dad would have started at Mount Lehman School in about 1930. I found a photo of the 1935 class at Mount Lehman School, which includes both Dad and his brother Jim (in the book "Heart of the Fraser Valley".

I found a note in Dad's materials referring to the team "Yell" at Mount Lehman School, written by Dad about 1936:

"Ripsaw, Ripsaw, Ripsaw, Bang!
We belong to a Mt. Lehman Gang!
Are we in it?
Well I guess!
Mt. Lehman, Mt. Lehman, YES! YES! YES!
M.O.U.N.T. L.E.H.M.A.N.
!!!MOUNT LEHMAN!!!"

As Dad and Uncle Jim got older, I am told that they would venture to their grandparents house to stay the weekend - I have mentioned this in previous chapters; this is when the good times with the grandparents, Uncle Gordy and Gordon Bretelle, took place. These weekend visits pressed an indelible stamp on Dad's upbringing, and he told me the stories for the rest of his life.

MT. LEHMAN SCHOOL CLASS 1935
Back row: Evelyn Israel (McMath), Eileen Simpson (McNeil), Eileen
Nicholson (Bidgood), Margaret Lehman, Martha Wishoff
Third row: Helen Israel (Dutka), Chesa Oye, Nellie Carter (Emery),
Sonia Savitsky (Collins), Marion McDonald, Nellie Coghlan, Mary
Oye, Kathleen Philps (Lamb)
Second row: Doug Redford, Ray Boury, John Carter, Albert Wishoff,
Jim Taylor, Howard Israel, Victor Sivitsky, John Tucker
Front row: Russel Nicholson, Dennie Moran, Izumi Tunyama, Jim
McDonald, Micky Moran, Teddy Redford, Doug Taylor, Gordon
McDonald

1935 photo of Dad's Mount Lehman School Class. He would have been 11 years old. Dad is in the bottom row, far right, with arms crossed.

As to Dad's secondary education, his notes indicate that he attended "Mount Lehman Superior School". I believe this is what was otherwise called Dunach School, located on the corner of Downes and Mount Lehman. This was also the location of Matsqui Municipal Hall prior to about 1953. I believe he may have attended at least Grade 11 there. I have his school yearbooks for Grades 12 and 13, at Philip Sheffield High School, which was then the only high school in the MSA area. (Parenthetically, I attended Abbotsford Senior High School in the 1960s, which was the only senior secondary school in the MSA District then.)

Dad, left, and his brother Jim, at the beach, probably White Rock.

Dad's Grade 12 graduating class, at Phillip Sheffield. He is in the second row from the back, three in from the right.

Philip Sheffield High School was located in Abbotsford. Dad must have been bused to high school from Mount Lehman. I have the school yearbook for the year 1940-1941. First, it mentions Dad as an art editor. As a comment about him, as a Grade 12 boy, it says:

"Douglas Taylor - Doug is kept busy drawing cartoons for school organizations." Later, under the heading of The Boys Cooking Club, it lists Dad as a member of the "Four Flap Jack Flippers", along with Donald Low, Sandy Purver and Philip Lehman.

Dad's cooking class at Phillip Sheffield - he is sitting on the top step, on the left.

In his Senior Matriculation year (Grade 13), the yearbook of 1941-1942 makes the following mentions of Dad:

- he is listed as the Class Representative of the Student's Council for Senior Matric;

- under the Class Comment section for Senior Matric: "*We'd like to congratulate Doug for the super cartoons on which he has spent much time during the year. He is also quite useful in holding up the argument in history period.*"

- under the Class Personnel section: "*Douglas Taylor - Doug is alert in mind, artistic in hand, We think his cartoons are really grand.*"

- he is listed as President of the Art Club, and secretary of the Badminton Club.

In Dad's later years, he became a politician. I wondered how, early in his life, his interest in politics started. I answered this question when I found notes about a book he intended to write, to be called "A Quarter Century in the Front Line", which he never finished, but I found some interesting notes about his early political thoughts, which he apparently began to have in the 1930s. The following is an example of his notes, under the heading "First Blood":

> "*I can recall having a few chores around a committee room during the Provincial Campaign about 1937, and attending a political meeting with my father shortly after, in Mission City, and I can also recall being a runner at committee rooms in 1940 or 1941. Gradually, interest was building and I was taking sides in high school. It seemed to me that many held the view that the country was all haywire and that the government owed people a living. The CCFers were peddling the line everywhere, in a publication called "The Stumprancher", and were distributing "Plenty for All" brand canned goods. I could*

not help but form an opinion, because the depression had been a problem in our family, and yet we were not complaining or agitating. In many cases the strong socialists were better off than we were and I could not help but think that in some cases they talked socialism to hide their own reasonable wealth.... Then on the completion of Senior Matriculation, at the age of 18, I joined the RCAF, and started to receive political material from the Progressive Conservative party. It was during this period that I studied the party policies and took great interest in the leadership of John Bracken. Here was acceptance by the Conservative party of a leader of the Progressive movement of the West, ...and the first influence in the party of John Diefenbaker. I also had the opportunity, in 1942, of a weekend leave, to the House of Commons in Ottawa, where I visited George Cruikshank, MP for Fraser Valley, and later in the war, I attended a Conservative Picnic where I heard John Bracken speak. I was able to cast my first ballot, an active service ballot, while under the age of 21."

**Dad's Senior Matric (Grade 13) class at Phillip Sheffield, June, 1942.
He is in the back row, far right.**

So in this chapter, I mention Dad's upbringing in Mount Lehman, his interests at school, and early mention of his interest in politics. A couple of other topics I wish to mention: first, his attendance at Mount Lehman United Church. Like me, he was baptized in the church, and attended Sunday school there. He likely had his grandmother Gaby Forrester as his teacher. He attended the church throughout his life, with his family, both before and after he married.

Another topic which must be mentioned is his handwriting. He was taught the McLean Method of handwriting in school, as were all other kids, as far as I know, but he made an art of it! I have never seen anyone else with such beautiful longhand writing skills. Maybe it went hand-in-hand with his ability to draw, but it was amazing. He told me that, as a child, he entered a sample of his handwriting at the Gifford Fair, and won a prize. And before I leave this topic, I should say that he was a prolific writer - I have hundreds of pages of his notes, written on various topics and in this beautiful handwriting, some of which I will mention in later chapters.

So we leave this chapter as Dad turns 18, in 1942. Dad had been pleading with Bap to let him sign on to the war effort by lying about his age (you had to be 18), but his father told him he had to wait until he was 18. So Dad continued on with his schooling and completed Senior Matric. But as soon as he turned 18, he signed up for the Royal Canadian Air Force, which will be one of the subjects of the next chapter.

BRIEF HISTORY OF MATSQUI UNIT 315

CHARTERED - MARCH 14, 1952 - BOX 123, McNEIL RD, MOUNT LEHMAN, B.C

Following World War I a branch of the Great War Veterans Assn was formed in Mount Lehman. It was formed about 1920 and met at the Orange Hall.

Prominent Members were:- Fred Carter (Boer War & WWI), Alfred Tucker (WWI), J.P. Carr (WWI), James Simpson (WWI), Cecil Gibson, M.M & Bar (WWI), P. Leslie Brice (WWI) Secretary, & Murdock Gillis D.C.M (WWI) & John Gray (WWI).

About 1930 amalgamated with MSA Branch 15 Royal Canadian Legion. Matsqui Veterans were active during the 30's and more so during the Second World War.

Fred Carter canvassed the whole West Matsqui area on foot during the war raising funds for servicemen. At the same time Cecil Gibson canvassed large businesses in New Westminster & Vancouver.

These 2 WW1 Veterans with WW2 Veterans held several organizational meetings in 1950 & 1951 in the Mt Lehman Orange Hall & received its Charter dated March 14, 1952.

Charter Members:- Clarence Emery, Cecil Gibson, Robert C Smith, Lee Spearman, Bert James, Gordon McDonald, Lorn Scott, John Tucker, Harold Black, Robert Merritt, Angus Ryder, L.W. Davis, Fergie Stratton, Joe Langton, Wes Coles, A.A. Holden, C.W Marsh, P.W. McCormick, L.W. Seward, J H Gray, James Simpson, Leonard P. Phelps, Fred Carter, Cecil Grinsted, R. McConachie, Gene Palmer, Bert Anderson, Bruce Stewart, Mel Glover, Sandy Purser, P. McConachie, Ron Grinsted, Wm Lucas, John Carter, Doug Taylor, George Baloc, Muriel Israel, James Taylor & Howard Israel.

The new Charter gave its jurisdiction as the District of Matsqui.

After leaving the Orange Hall for 10 years, in 1961 the Club purchased a Heritage Wartime Building at Abbotsford airport and moved it to a site on McNeil Road donated by the McNeil Family & the Taylor Family with the subdivision approval by Matsqui Municipality.

This is a sample of Dad's handwriting - a portion of his notes on the history of Unit 315, Army, Navy, and Air Force Veterans Club.

Chapter 6

A LIFETIME OF SERVICE

Dad in RCAF unform.

Once again, Dad's notes are invaluable. He must really have enjoyed military service, as he belonged to five different military or paramilitary organizations at various times in his life, namely:

1. The Royal Canadian Air Force

Another photo of Dad in RCAF uniform.

Dad signed up for service on August 12, 1942. He was assigned to 133 Fighter Squadron, as an Air Frame Mechanic. He really wanted to train as a pilot, but he was disqualified, as he was colour-blind. (Our son, Ryan, has trained and works as a pilot for Air Canada - and currently flies a Boeing 777. Dad would have been so proud to know this!) I believe Dad initially took his training as an Air Frame Mechanic at Boundary Bay Airport in Delta, BC. His job involved repairing and maintaining the frames of aircraft, many of which were made of fabric and wood in that era.

Another job, which I'm sure he loved more, was as Art Editor of the first RCAF Newspaper in Western Air Command.

Dad spent over three years in the RCAF, with many postings. Some places to which he was posted included Boundary Bay and Tofino, BC, St. Thomas, Ontario, and Mont Joli, Quebec, (on the Gaspe Peninsula.)

2. Mount Lehman 1922 Cadet Corps

Following discharge from the RCAF, Dad was appointed Chief Training Officer of Mount Lehman 1922 Cadet Corps, from 1946 to 1948, which was located at Abbotsford Airport. I believe it was affiliated with the Royal Westminster Regiment.

3. The Westminster Regiment (later renamed The Royal Westminster Regiment.)

After his stint as Chief Training Officer of the Cadet Corps, from September 1, 1946 to October, 1948, he transferred to "B" Company of the Regiment, where he served in this militia unit from September, 1949 to January, 1967. Thus, he spent almost 25 years in military service to Canada.

The headquarters of the Royal Westminster was, and still is, at 6th and Queen's Street, in New Westminster. I remember the armouries fondly, as we would attend the Christmas parties there when we were kids - complete with a visit from Santa, gifts, and festive music by the Regimental band.

Dad and Uncle Jim were both active in the Regiment down through those years. I know Dad was the Company Sergeant Major at one point, and would parade both at New Westminster, and at Mission. I remember his loud voice bellowing out orders to the marching men. We would frequently, as a family, attend at the Mission City Remembrance Day Ceremonies, and watch Dad lead the regiment down First Avenue, Mission, to the cenotaph.

Dad left the Royal Westminster Regiment, in 1967, with the rank of Lieutenant. Dad's war and service medals included: Canadian Voluntary Service Medal, (C.V.S.M.,) Defense Medal, (D.M.,) Canada Forces Decoration, (C.D). In addition to the medals mentioned above, the fourth medal he wore, on special occasions such as Remembrance Day, was the Centennial Medal, struck in 1967, to commemorate Canada's 100th birthday - about 20,000 of these medals were given to Canadian servicemen.

Dad in uniform as Sergeant Major in the Royal Westminster Regiment.

Dad, as Mayor of Matsqui, in May, 1971, inspecting members of his former
regiment, the Royal Westminster Regiment, following the investiture of the
regiment with "Freedom of the Municipality". Col. L. Deane, Commanding Officer,
is to Dad's right.

When Dad was Mayor of the Municipality of Matsqui, the Royal Westminster Regiment was given the distinction "Freedom of the District of Matsqui", and the Regiment marched to the Municipal Hall to receive the award. This was 8 May, 1971, the same day as the Royal Visit of Her Majesty Queen Elizabeth II (with a ceremony at Abbotsford Airport, which was in Matsqui Municipality.)

4. Auxiliary member to the Matsqui Police Force, 1950s.

Dad's father was instrumental, while on Matsqui Council, in Matsqui establishing its own municipal police force, in the mid-1950s.

Then Dad and Uncle Jim joined the auxiliary unit of the force, basically to assist the regular police force members. They were involved in the auxiliary for several years.

So Dad started out as an auxiliary member of the force, in the mid 50s, and later, as Mayor of Matsqui Municipality, he served as the Chairman of the Matsqui Police Board. In fact, when Dad left the Police Board Chairman's job, he was presented with a miniature Matsqui Police Badge, which he always carried in his wallet.

Dad (as Mayor of the Municipality) meeting the Queen at Abbotsford Airport. Prince Philip just behind the Queen. Mum is to Dad's right.

5. Hall #5, Matsqui Volunteer Fire Department.

Dad was involved in Hall #5 on many levels. In 1968, Dad was Mayor of the Municipality of Matsqui. Mount Lehman/Bradner area had no local fire hall, so Dad made provision to establish a temporary hall. Initially, Mount Lehman Volunteer Fire Hall #5 was established and located at the Cargill Hog Farm on Landing Road. The first fire truck was a 1946 Ford.

In 1973 the fire truck was relocated to the Taylors Farm Service garage, while a new Mount Lehman Fire Hall was built. The new fire hall and library was completed in 1974. The fire hall had one truck bay. Later an additional truck bay was added for a pumper truck.

In 1976, Dad joined Hall #5 as a volunteer fire-fighter. As his insurance office was in close proximity to the hall, he was quite often the first hall member to attend at Hall #5 to ready the fire equipment to proceed to the fire call, or to drive the truck himself to the call location. My brother Grant says that when Dad's pager went off, he immediately shot out of his office at a run.

Hall #5, Mount Lehman Fire Hall (on the right of this building); Mount Lehman Library is on the left. Dad was responsible for establishing both the Fire Hall and the Library, while Mayor of Matsqui, in 1974.

Dad and our daughter Karen in one of the Mount Lehman fire trucks.

Dad continued to serve on Hall #5 for approximately 15 years, eventually retiring as a Fire Captain.

Chapter 7

BUSINESS AND FAMILY IN MOUNT LEHMAN

This chapter is about Dad's return to Mount Lehman after his service in the RCAF. It was fortunate that Dad left me very good notes about establishing his businesses, and I can do no better than to quote from his notes, which are quoted verbatim, in italics:

"On November 8, 1945, eight days after receiving my discharge from the RCAF, I took out a business licence, with the Municipality of Matsqui, as a General Merchant and Feed Delivery Service.

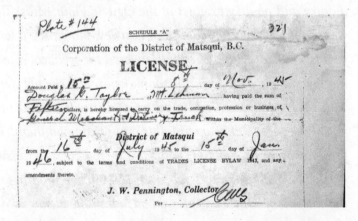

Dad's first business license. This license is for "General Merchant and Delivery Truck."

My father had written me prior to my release that an opening for a Miracle Feed Dealership was available in the west Matsqui area. It was this letter that made the decision for me as to whether I would take my discharge that was offered to me, from the RCAF, or whether I would accept a promotion and a 2-year occupation stint in Germany. While Mont Joli, Quebec, was a good station, and Germany was inviting, the war was the only reason for me being in the services, and since the war was over I had no intention of making the RCAF my career.

Returning to British Columbia was foremost on my mind and with so many servicemen returning it was an opportunity to get into business by myself and not have to compete in the job market. I purchased a piece of property adjacent to Mount Lehman United Church and proceeded to build a small store and warehouse.

The problem was that I had very little money, having saved only $1,400.00 during my Air Force service. So I went around and took orders for Miracle Feeds, which was a trade name for a dairy and poultry product of the Ogilvie Flour Mills. Then I went to the Ogilvie warehouse in Langley, purchased a load of feed from them with a cheque, delivered the feed, collected the money and deposited it in the bank before the cheque cleared! Miracle Feeds was a good product and it was packed in 100 lb. cotton bags with colourful dots and writing on them. These products were in demand, and sales increased. Veterans were given some assistance; I received $60.00 per month for 12 months, all of which was plowed back into the business.

Dad's first business (with Uncle Jim as his partner), was located just south of Mount Lehman United Church. On the left is the Ford Delivery Truck, with Dad behind the wheel, and on the right two views of the store building. This building was later moved to become a part of the new store building at 5913 Mount Lehman Road.

I also had an opportunity to purchase a war surplus truck. It was to be supplied through Abbotsford Motors, and I had made a down payment and entered into a contract to acquire the vehicle over time. The truck never arrived, so I pressed Abbotsford Motors every few days for several months, to no avail. So I had to buy a black market truck, a 1946 Ford 2-ton, for $2,000 -the war surplus truck was to have been $900.

A year later, I was in the Mount Lehman Post Office, when a collector came in looking for me. He asked me why I was behind in my payments on the truck that I had purchased from

Abbotsford Motors. I explained to him what happened and that I had not received the truck, and after investigation they found that Abbotsford Motors had sold the war surplus truck to someone else, for a higher price, but had kept my deposit and obtained the money from the finance company (the contract in my name). I believe this was a criminal act, which cost me the deposit paid and considerable inconvenience.

My brother Jim decided to come into the business with me, and contributed $850.00, and we were able to work together for many years. We were in pretty good physical shape in those days - one time we unloaded 150 tons of feed in a day and a half. One summer, we purchased, trucked and sold several hundred ton of hay. It was a tough business and the profit was small - hardly enough on which to raise our families.

However, we expanded into the general merchandising business, at the little store adjacent to the Church - I even cut hair for .25 per head. I thought nothing of buying a short hip of beef and cutting steaks and roasts from it. We became a Shell Canada dealer in April of 1946, which rounded out the business.

I had applied for the Shell Canada dealership as soon as I returned home from the RCAF. In the Spring of 1946, my friend Len Philps, who had just come home from the Army, engineered the simple building on the lot I bought next to the church, and it seemed no time and progress was made. I remember we were shingling the roof of the building, and who did we see walking down Mount Lehman Road, in uniform, carrying his kit bag, none other than Howard Israel (whose family farm was across the street from the church)- home from the war, and for good!

At first we stocked the warehouse with a line of animal feeds that seemed to be marketable. Dairy and poultry feeds, stock salt, hay salt and some wheat, bran, barley chop, etc. Then we made a deal with Otter Co-op for coal, barbed wire, utensils, garden tools, and so on. So with sales of gasoline and oil, as well as the farm supplies, we had a fair stock of merchandise.

Growth was hard on our finances, because we refused to take a bank loan for stock, and as we added more and more goods for sale, it had to be paid for in cold cash. Because of this, my brother and I took a side contract with Ogilvie's in Cloverdale, unloading 50 ton box-cars of feed for .75 per ton. We did this for a couple of years and although it was hard work, it stabilized our business.

My wife Elsie was a tremendous help right from the start. Jim's wife Ellen had two little girls to look after, which occupied much of her time.

In 1947, fire destroyed the Malcolm MacAskill Store, home, and feed warehouse, which was located on the west side of Mount Lehman Road, just north of the BC Electric Railway tracks. When we learned that the Macaskills didn't own the property and that it was not to be re-built, my father, Buster Taylor, said that he would go to the owner, Harry Fowles, in White Rock, and make him an offer for the property. We purchased the property for $500 (with father's money), and at that time Taylors Farm Service was born, with the shares being equal among Jim, myself and our father. We decided to build a new store, of a size of 30 x 50 ft, and engaged Dave and Frank

Neufeld, who contracted to build it for $3,500, and completed it in 1948.

In 1947, we had built a feed warehouse at Dennison railway siding - it was a 20 x 50ft warehouse. My father had offered Elsie and I timber from the back of his farm to build a house, but we took the timber for lumber for the warehouse instead. Lightbaum Brothers had set up a small mill on Taylor Road East, where they cut the logs into lumber for us. These brothers had both been in the RCAF as pilots overseas, and formerly had been from Mission. We had become friendly with them, and I remember one time transporting a small building for them to live in. We hauled it by truck!

We delivered merchandise on a weekly basis, making some 30 or 40 deliveries. In those days there were at least a dozen farmers shipping milk from McTavish Road and Marsh-McCormick Roads. Jimmy Allan was at the end of our route, on Allan Road (an extension of Marsh-McCormick Road). He was an old countryman, who served in the Royal Flying Corps in the First World War, as a rigger and fitter (the same job I had in the second war). He was at a training school in the southern U.S. towards the end of the war, which was established to train Americans. He certainly was a character. He ordered loads of canned foods from us, and just threw the empty cans out his kitchen window. What a pile of cans there was after 30 years! When he died, he left his place to the Loyal Orange Protestant Home, and I was asked by the directors of the home for advice on its disposal. He had milked about 4 or 5 cows by hand, and shipped the milk by 10 gallon cans, as was the practise in those days.

Clarence Marsh was another dairy farmer. His father had settled in Jubilee in 1881-2. Clarence was born and raised on the farm.

Patrick William (Bill) McCormick was the most influential and best loved pioneer of the Jubilee area. He was born and raised on the farm, and milked cows all his life. He was a bachelor, who gave advice to all the young men in Jubilee. He told me many stories of pioneer days.

Matt Susani was a logger, but farmed as well, in later years, and was always a friendly face on the delivery route.

Walter Thrower, another dairy farmer on Satchell Road, was a hardy dairy farmer.

Louis W. Stewart was a poultryman and dairy farmer; few people had the understanding of the poultry business and husbandry as he did.

One of the real pioneers, who lived across from the Stewarts, was one of the best calls on my route. Art Boyle and Mrs. Boyle were delightful people. I shall never forget being asked to stay for tea. The long wooden table had served so many people and kids with the nicest treats, by the nicest people. Art Boyle's father had bought the old Lee farm for $50.00 and 2 sacks of flour.

Jack Gray had a small farm, but I never saw any evidence of farming. He was a World War I veteran that had seen quite a bit of action. He was a piano player and entertained at the Army and Navy & Airforce Veterans' Club, when the Club first met at the Orange Hall.

Billy Satchell, who lived across from Boyles', moved on to Satchell Road about 1910 or so, or at least his father did. They were good neighbours, and although they went through hard times and hard luck, they still remained cheerful. My Dad told me that Satchells lost most of their cattle one time with an affliction called "Red Water".

John Carter was a World War II veteran, who lived on the corner of Ross and Taylor Road. He served with the Calgary Highlanders, and was wounded four times. When he settled on his farm (he obtained it under the provisions of the Veterans' Land Act), and one time was digging in his garden, he found some bottles of saki that the Japanese had buried, when they were evacuated. Len Philps, John and I sat in John's kitchen one summer evening in 1946, and sampled the rice drink.

Next door to John Carter was Leonard Philps, also a WW2 veteran; who was wounded after D-Day in the push through Holland to Germany. He was also a dairyman, and had settled under the Veterans' Land Act.

Across from Len Philps was his father's farm. His father, William B Philps, had a mixed farm; he was also an excellent horse-driver and horse handler. He was born and raised in a central British town. He swore that a Taylor he knew back home was the spitting image of my Dad's Uncle Herb. Billy Philps was a very happy and kindly person, even though it was a tough go in his early days in Mount Lehman. I always made his farm the last stop on my deliveries, because he made such delicious bread pudding that I couldn't resist sampling it whenever possible. His son, Fred Philps, a Navy Veteran, took over his Dad's farm, and expanded the dairy business.

The above are but a few of the friendly people that we visited on delivery days -others will be mentioned in other stories.

When I canvass my memory of my life prior to the war, my focus was the area surrounding the Mount Lehman School. In those days, we didn't travel much, so the people we knew best lived close to where we lived.

We had many Japanese families in Mount Lehman before WWII. They were good neighbours, and very industrious people. They mostly farmed strawberries and raspberries. Our neighbour across Taylor Road was the Taniyama family. Shigeru and Izumi were my closest boyhood friends. We played together continuously from my age about 6-16. We fished Nicholson Creek, and the Fraser River; we built tree houses and fern houses and played marbles to and from school. We also had many variations of hoops, stilts and kites. The last time I saw them was one time I was home on leave, and they were packing their belongings onto a truck, and then we said goodbye to each other. Shigeru turned to me and said "If you have anything to do with us after the war, don't send us to Japan because my father left there in 1904 and we have no connection there." Unfortunately, I never saw them again, although one day in the early 50's I was driving out Ross Road to the corner of Downes Road, and I saw a Japanese fellow working in the field. I stopped and walked over to him, and asked if he had any idea where the Taniyama boys were. He said he didn't but suggested that I get in touch with a Japanese newspaper in Vancouver, and maybe they could help. When I got back to the store in about 10-15 minutes, my Dad and brother Jim had had a short visit from Izumi Taniyama. He could not wait for me as he was travelling to Kamloops with a carload of people who were anxious to get moving. Alas! I had missed him, and never saw him again.

As I said, there were a number of Japanese families in the Mount Lehman area before WWII. There was "Yama," who lived on the farm later acquired by Len Philps after the war. Yama was a Japanese military officer who freely predicted he would own our property some day. He and my Uncle Gordy were friendly but Gordy got into many arguments with him. The RCMP searched his farm and found evidence that he was a Japanese officer, Other Japanese families: Kimamotos, Nadas Oyes, Ogatas, to mention a few more.

I even attended Japanese school, and had at least a 500 word Japanese vocabulary at the time. The Japanese School and Hall was built on the corner of the Yama (Len Philps) property on Ross Road. The Japanese people were good community supporters and good neighbours.

I have always had the feeling that the government should be prepared to offer some compensation for the seizure of the Japanese familys' property, and, although it was a very dangerous time for us on the West Coast after Pearl Harbour, and the occupation of the Aleutian Islands by the Japanese, and I believe the Canadian government was arguably justified to take the action that it did; nevertheless Canadians/British Subjects (as the majority of the Japanese were), were not fairly compensated. All the Japanese properties in the Mount Lehman area were taken over by the government and allotted to returning war veterans. I chose not to take up the 40 acres on Mount Lehman Road, running from Spallin Ave to Mount

Lehman Motors. Although my name was written on the VLA map and the price was right ($1,100), one of the reasons that I didn't take it was that I felt an injustice had been done and I did not want it on my conscience.

The operation of our mixed merchandising business involved pumping gas at the old pump, by filling the glass part of the upright pump by a back and forth hand pumping motion. The glass contained 10 gallons of gasoline. Then we also had feed sales - all in 100 lb sacks and in the first store, we had a modest supply of groceries, and a bit of hardware. Initially we had no counter-fridges, but had a Coca-Cola cooler that we used dry of water and cranked it down cold. As fresh meat only came in on Wednesday, I would have steaks, chops and roasts cut (by myself) for specific orders and extra sales. For example, Hugh Gillis, a pioneer farmer, who was born in Mount Lehman, had a special roast beef order every week. Mrs. Percy Carr (one of the Mount Lehman pioneers) whose husband Percy was a double amputee from injuries received in WWI, had a standing order of a rib roast, weekly, for many years.

(As an aside, it was Sgt. Murdoch Gillis, DCM, who was in no mans' land overseas during WWI, when he came upon a mass of dead soldiers. He heard groaning coming from the mass of soldiers he thought dead. He picked that soldier up and carried him back to friendly territory. The soldier he saved was Percy Carr.)

Richard Owen, and his daughters, Misses Ruth and Lucy Owen, patronized our business. Mr. Owen was a farmer and a horticulturalist. He made butter and shipped vegetables, butter and cream by River Boat to the New Westminster market.

He also developed a new strain of strawberries, British Royal Sovereign, which proved to be very popular. He made excellent apple cider, and a visit with him gave us the opportunity to sample some. Mr. Owen was responsible for the establishment of the Matsqui Agricultural and Horticultural Association, and was its first President. (My uncle, John Taylor, was a first Director) and it had its first fair at Gifford, in 1911. It was the forerunner of the Central Fraser Valley Fair.

I had earlier referred to us building the Dennison warehouse (on Dennison Road, now called Ross Road, at the tracks). I had acquired a lease, at a cost of $10.00 per month, on the property adjacent to the siding. We decided that we would have a party for the official opening of the warehouse. Corny Penner, with a fiddle, and another fellow with an accordion, provided some music, and it was on my 23rd birthday, May 31, 1947, at that party, that Elsie and I announced our engagement, the wedding to be held on July 16, 1947.

(Author's note: My mother, formerly Elsie Wall, grew up in Saskatchewan, and moved to BC with her family in 1942. An excellent source of Mum's family history is contained in her brother (Ben Wall's) 1992 book, called "Walls With Strong Foundations", a copy of which I have in my library. I have also conducted research into Grandma Wall's (Mum's mother's) family. In 2019, Sharon and I travelled to Poland and visited the town of Rynsk, where Grandma Wall grew up. There we found the church, in Rynsk, where Grandma Wall's mother was married. In 1913, the family moved to Saskatchewan, where she eventually met my grandfather, John Wall, and they raised their family on a small farm near Herbert, Saskatchewan.)

The next year, 1948, marked the opening of the new store, at 5913 Mount Lehman Road, across the tracks from Mount Lehman Credit Union. We had a modern facility, far better than the old store next to Mount Lehman United Church. We had far more space, and more modern refrigeration equipment. The community responded positively to our new venture, and gave us their loyal patronage for many years to come.

This is the store building, from 1948. There was also a feed shed on the left (south) side of the building.

I do not seem to have a photo of the feedshed, which was formerly attached on the south side of the building.

In 1947, we had become the distributor for Quaker Flour and Quaker Oats, supplying Flour and Cereals to many Fraser Valley stores, including Yarrow and Deroche to the east, and Milner to the west. In the 1948 flood of the Fraser, Quaker

Oats contracted us to take a load of flour from Chilliwack to the docks in Vancouver, bound for Victoria.

The salesman for Quaker Oats did his circuit of the various stores, and took the orders, and we delivered them. We had access to the prices being charged by Quaker on its invoices, and because of this knowledge, I became interested in politics, which I will explain further later on.

After three years, we found out that Quaker Oats was paying a company called Westminster Storage and Distributors 3 times the freight fee that they were paying us. I told them that if they didn't increase our commission to equal what they were paying Westminster Storage, and back-date it, we would quit the contract. They didn't and we did. We then closed the Dennison warehouse.

We then got a moving company to move the Dennison warehouse, the mile east to our new store location on Mount Lehman Road, and we placed it beside our new store building, to become the automotive garage. We contracted with Nels Olund, a local contractor, to install the foundation, and adapt the old warehouse to the new concrete foundation. Nels Olund was a very well-respected contractor, which we already knew. (When my Grandfather's house burned down in 1910, Nels Olund had come to see him and said, "Taylor, if you give me $2,000 cash, I will build you the best house in the country". They hired him, and the house was very good, and lasted them for their lifetime. This was the home of the family of Edward and Elizabeth Taylor (my grandfather and grandmother), and their children Gordon, Henry (my Dad, called "Buster") and Kitty.

So the new building, built by the Neufelds, was the central portion of the building; the old feed warehouse became the automotive shop (to be operated by my father, Buster Taylor), and the feed warehouse, the building which had formerly been our old store adjacent to the church, was attached on the south side, to become our feed warehouse. We had a modern store complex, and with my brother Jim, and my father Buster, we were ready to expand our business.

I also purchased a general insurance business from a Matsqui gentleman, Alex Bates, in 1949, and carried on the insurance business, including general insurance and auto, in a portion of the store building, as well.

All three of us operated the general merchant's business (which we later operated through a limited company called Taylors Farm Service Ltd) from 1948 to 1961, when my brother Jim took over the dairy farm operation on the original Taylor homestead on Taylor Road (following the untimely death of my uncle, Gordy Taylor, in 1959). My Dad and I continued in the business until his death, from cancer, in 1966.

Because of my involvement in Municipal politics, following the death of my father, in 1966, (who, at the time, was a Matsqui Municipal Councillor) my wife Elsie, with the help of my children, Gordon, Grant, Rosemary and Douglas, continued to operate the general merchandise business until 1976. In that year, we decided to rent out a portion of the building, which became a restaurant. I continued to operate the insurance office, and the automotive garage was rented out to several tenants. Doug Olson was, by far, the longest and best tenant, having served the people of Mount Lehman since 1980.

In 1980, my son Grant joined my insurance business for a period of 5 years, at which time he was offered the position of Manager of Mutual Fire Insurance Company of British Columbia. He accepted the position with Mutual Fire, and enjoyed a long period of employment with that firm as its CEO. In 1984, my youngest son, Douglas Jr., took over the business, and continues to operate it to the present."

Dad's notes, quoted above, describe how he established his businesses in Mount Lehman. An earlier chapter told how my great-grandmother, Gaby Forrester, turned over her house to Dad and Mum. This happened about 1949. I arrived in the world in that year, and my three siblings followed: Grant in 1952, Rosemary in 1955, and Doug Jr. in 1962. The house at 6184 Mount Lehman Road was quite large and easily accommodated our family. It was a five-acre property, and we had, at various times, a milk-cow, calves, pigs (named Grant and Gordon) and several horses. Grant and I helped Dad and Mum with farm chores; Mum even churned butter for our family's use. We had a very pleasant childhood, growing up in that house.

As outlined in Gordon Bretelle's earlier notes, Dad was very inventive in making things, especially bows and arrows, and sling-shots. Dad had so much patience with these little tasks, carefully cutting shafts for arrows out of cedar, collecting feathers and inserting them into slots on the arrows (to make them fly true) and attaching weights on the tip. Also he showed Grant and I how to make slingshots, either out of rubber or leather - whatever we had at hand. Then we would craft makeshift targets, and have competitions! Another fun activity with Dad was making kites from scratch. In those days, we either could not buy ready-made kites, or couldn't afford them, so Dad taught Grant and I how to make them out of newspaper, string and light wood strips as a frame. We also made the kite tails out of newspaper. These kites flew very well, and occupied us for hours at a time.

Another activity with Dad was fishing down in the gullies leading to the river. We would drive to the very end of Schroeder Road, park our car, and then we would descend down into the huge ravine. We would bring along from home a fishing line and hook, and we would wrap that around a small stick. When we got to the bottom of the ravine, we would walk along the creek, through the thick brush, until we found a little area in the creek which formed a pond; we would then cut a fishing pole from the bush, and attach it to the line we brought. We then fished in those little pools.

We give prompt personal Autoplan Service!

also complete
- HOME
- TENANT
- FARM
- BUSINESS
- TRAVEL
- LIABILITY
- INSURANCE

DOUGLAS G. TAYLOR
General Insurance Agents

office: 5913 Mt. Lehman Rd. North
Mount Lehman

Phones: **856-2818**
and
856-2133

— Since 1949 —

This is a sample of a brochure which Dad had printed, to advertise his insurance business. He had bought the general insurance business in 1949 from a Mr. Bates, a Matsqui Prairie resident.

As I got older, I would help up at the store, with selling feed, gas, or helping Bap at the garage. I would get off the school bus at the store, and spend until closing time pumping gas, loading feed, or selling groceries. Another job soon devolved to me when I got my driver's license, namely driving the delivery truck (a 1950 Chev 1-ton flat-deck, the first vehicle I was allowed to drive), delivering feed and groceries to some of those same people referred to by Dad in his notes above.

This is the type of advertising Dad would send out to the Mount Lehman community. Note the "Centennial Memo".

This is a Sunday school photo of Mount Lehman United Church, circa 1955. You will see me, with a bow-tie, about mid-photo peaking out from the second row. My brother Grant, aged about 4, in in the front row, second from right.

Mum was very active in the church, which was two doors north of our home. Each of us kids was baptized there, and attended Sunday school.

After Bap died in 1966, Dad gradually took over more of the farm responsibilities on Taylor Road, to assist Granny, who was 65 when Bap died. Then Granny decided to turn over the farm to Mum and Dad, and they decided to build a new home, in 1969, next door to the old Burton/Anna/John house. They then moved into that house; Dad qualified for a Veterans Land Act loan (as a former active serviceman). Dad then acquired a Massey Ferguson 35 tractor, and some farm machinery, and took on yet another business - that of raising a herd of Hereford beef cattle. (By 1969, I lived at UBC, and never really lived in the new house, except I stayed there when home from university.)

Mum's jobs and responsibilities, in addition to all her child-raising ones, were to assist in the store business, until about 1976, and later to help with the insurance business, which became busier and busier when they got an ICBC Autoplan license in 1973, and also as Dad took on more and more responsibility in elected office. And of course, living on the farm, Mum assisted with farm chores as well - never a dull moment!

In 1971, the year Sharon and I got married, I was just starting law school. Sharon had a degree in Education, from UBC, and got a job at School District #34 in Abbotsford. I was in first year law school. So I was commuting from our apartment in New Westminster to UBC and Sharon was commuting to Abbotsford each day. One day we were talking to Mum on the phone, and she said she was helping Granny clean up the old house, at 30004 Taylor, so they could rent it out again. Sharon and I discussed the situation, and decided we were needier than any tenant they could find, so we gave up our apartment, and moved into the old house, where we lived for 9 years. It was then an easy commute for Sharon to get to her school, and I made an arrangement with a neighbour, Jack Ferguson, to travel, first to 264th and the freeway, with Jack, and then by commuter buses, to UBC. These were long days! You wouldn't think of doing this today.

My sister, Rosemary, attended UBC as well, attaining a teacher's degree, and spent her working life at schools in Langley. My brother, Grant spent some time in the Okanagan, and then returned to Mount Lehman in 1980 to work with Dad in his insurance business, for a period of five years. Grant moved into the old house after Sharon and I built our new house on Burgess Road, in 1980. My brother Doug later worked with Dad in his insurance business, and took it over upon Dad's death in 1998.

I should mention that Mum and Dad caught the travel bug early in the 1970s. I remember they joined a travel club, called Air Club International, which owned one or two jets, and flew to Hawaii and Mexico. Dad signed up, and we started to fly with Air Club. I believe the first time they travelled on Air Club, they took us all to Hawaii. After that, they started to travel to Mexico, first with Air Club, and then with other carriers. Their favourite destination was Puerto Vallerta, and specifically the Tropicana Hotel in old downtown. They would arrange to go to Mexico on a moment's notice, then fax the Tropicana for a couple of night's reservation, and then, once they got to PV, they would extend their stay, if desired. I believe Mum and Dad had been to Mexico 71 times by the time Dad passed away. They just loved Mexico and the Mexican people - they made fast Mexican and other friends there; they even babysat for their Mexican friends while they were there. And Dad so enjoyed drawing and painting - we have so many examples of his artwork, the subjects of which, in many cases, originated in Mexico.

Before leaving the topic of Mexico, I will mention that about 1989 or so, Dad saw a notice in the Mount Lehman Post Office, advertising the rental of a condo in San Jose del Cabo, in the Baja. He answered the ad, and it turned out that a couple in Bradner had a condo there, and later two condos there, and we started going to the Baja, instead of PV. At times, we rented the two condos, one for Mum and Dad, one for us. In 1992, Sharon and I bought a condo in San Jose, with partners, and Mum and Dad would rent another unit in our complex, and we then continued to enjoy Mexico from this new location. Dad enjoyed the new location just as he had PV, and Mum and Dad also continued going to PV with Grant and Carol; he enjoyed fishing at both places, and also, of course, had his paints at the ready!

Mum and Dad also travelled a lot within BC and Canada, especially with the BC Municipal conventions, and Progressive Conservative conventions; they also travelled to Europe on tours (at least one trip with Olga and Glen, Mum's sister and her husband).

I can't forget to relate the stories about Loon Lake (a lake in the BC Interior, near Cache Creek). I do not know how the tradition started, but my mother's family, the Wall family, started to go fishing at Loon Lake about 1960, and that tradition continued with a fishing derby and family camping/cabin/motor home weekend, usually on the Father's Day weekend each year. It was a great time for all of us, and a chance to renew acquaintances with Mum's two brothers, Ben and John, and her sister, Olga, and families. We all looked forward to it each year.

But one year, Dad phoned me at work, in 1989, and said that he heard that a waterfront lot on Loon Lake was for sale, and he wanted me to go in on the purchase. It was a 100' by 200' lot and was available for $22,000. I said I was interested, and we bought it.

We enjoyed that lot, on which we located several RVs, and started to go up to Loon even more often than we had previously. Dad was an avid fisherman; so he bought a boat, we installed a wharf, and it became another one of Dad's interests, namely planning fishing trips with all the family, planning jobs on the lot, etc.

Speaking of Dad and fishing, yet another of his favourite activities was fishing at the Fraser River. We would fish with "bar rigs", a rod with a line on which two hooks were suspended, with a sinker on the end of the line. The bait was freshly dug worms, from our farm. To throw out the line to fish, you spun the bar rig in the air a few times, and flung it out into the river as far as you could. You then rested your rod on a y-shaped stick, and waited for the big one (hopefully sturgeon) to hit. We would make this a family activity day at either Duncan Bar in Glen Valley or the end of Landing Road (the former Lehman's Landing).

I forgot to tell you about casinos; Mum and Dad became gambling afficionados. Once again, I don't know where this interest started, but they enjoyed the casino, Reno, Vegas, and everything in between.

Mum and Dad lived happily in the new house on Taylor Road until Dad's death. Before Dad's death, Grant assisted Dad in the running of the farm, and added apple and blueberry orchards. Throughout Dad's life, he liked nothing better than driving his tractor, and clipping weeds or blackberries with his mower on his tractor - he said he did his best thinking while on his tractor. Mum continues to live in the "new" house to this day.

Sharon and I bought a new 27′ Maxum power boat in 1997, the year before Dad died. In the summer of that year, we took them on a tour of Indian Arm. From L to R - Karen, Mum, Dad and Ryan.

Dad and his brother Jim, photo taken shortly before Dad died in 1998.

Dad's insurance office was located at the south end of the store building. When the grocery, feed and car repair business was operating, his insurance business area was located in the north end of this building, near the garage.

Mum and Dad, at the celebration of their 50th Wedding Anniversary in 1997, just the year before he died.

Dad with our son Ryan, showing off their day's catch at Loon Lake.

Dad at his insurance office desk.

Dad and Gordon Bretelle. Gordon (my namesake, and we also shared birthdays), was Aunt Kitty's son. He was the fellow who gave us his notes about various family members, which I have shared in this book.

The Taylors Farm Service property at 5913 Mount Lehman Road was retained by my mother Elsie until 2022, and was then sold. The new owners removed the building in September, 2022- it had served our family for 74 years.

The next chapter details the various clubs and activities enjoyed by Dad during his life in Mount Lehman.

Chapter 8

DAD'S MOUNT LEHMAN CLUBS AND ACTIVITIES

You have probably noticed that Dad led a busy, (no, hectic), life. I have mentioned in previous chapters some of the clubs and organizations to which he belonged. I thought in this chapter I would mention some of the others:

1. Matsqui Unit 315, Army, Navy and Airforce Veterans in Canada -Mount Lehman

Dad was a charter member of Unit 315, as was his brother Jim: The Charter was issued on March 14, 1952. Dad was also President for a time, and Treasurer for about 40 years. In early years, the club met at the Mount Lehman Orange Hall. In 1960, the Taylors donated a parcel of land (which was a part of the Taylors Farm Service property), and Chester and Eileen McNeil also donated a parcel of their land, and the club purchased a former WWII building, situated at Abbotsford Airport, and had the building moved the approximate 8 kilometres to the site. I remember this day well (as a 12-year-old), - seeing club member Len Dumont on the top of the building, raising the hydro and telephone wires as it went along. From that time onward, the veterans of the area had their own local clubrooms, which formed the centre of their social life. As they had at their clubrooms in the Orange Hall, since 1952, they held regular social evenings, dances, whist and crib drives, and other activities, as well as their business meetings, throughout the year.

In the 1990s, Dad, Uncle Jim, and others, were concerned that Mount Lehman had no cenotaph, at which to commemorate Remembrance Day in November of each year. So, in 1992, the veterans in Mount Lehman built a cenotaph. Dad's notes, contained in the program of the dedication ceremony, for which he was Master of Ceremonies, held on September 26, 1992, are as follows:

> "The Cenotaph Project commenced in 1989, the committee being led by Leonard C. Philps. His design for the Cenotaph was, after his passing, followed by Ben Otto. They both deserve mention for their hard work and inspiration."

Dad's notes, containing a brief history of Matsqui Unit 315, are attached as Appendix 5 to this book.

2. The Lodges (Masonic and the Loyal Orange Lodge).

I know Dad was a Mason, but I don't have details of that membership. But I do have good notes of the Loyal Orange Lodge, #1868, left in Dad's impeccable handwriting:

> "The early Mount Lehman Pioneers had one thing in common: they were strong Protestants. Many had come from Ontario and the Maritimes where the Orange Association was strong.
> The need for a community hall, other than the small school, was pressing. LOL #1868 was formed, and in 1904 the Orange

Hall was built at the corner of Taylor and Mount Lehman Road. The so-called 'Porch Book' indicates that the following became members 1905 and 1906: W.J. Marsh, Jas. A. Ryder, Chas. A. Lindsay, Angus McLean, Lawrence Coghlan, Sam R. Nicholson, Dan B. McDougall, George McCallum, Jas. Merryfield, Neil Craig, Henry J. Ryder, James Towlan, William Merryfield, Daniel Nicholson, Eurvan Israel, Albert Israel, Malcolm D Morrison, Walter Towlan and Wm McEachern. The hall was built by volunteer labour, and dances were held to finish the project. Its use was no different than any community hall - the Orangemen rented the hall at a low rate, to anyone who wished it. The Lodge room was upstairs, seating 50-60 and was often full, especially when the County Lodge meetings were held here.

My father, H.E. Buster Taylor, became an Orangeman in the early 20s, and I in November, 1945. What a great opportunity this was for a young man like myself to be admitted to this age-old association, with local pioneers like Dan Nicholson, Hugh Gillis, Robert Hanna VC, Alex Bates, Eurvan Israel, Albert Israel, Cliff Israel, Bill Spallin, and later James Taylor, Len Philps, John Carter, Fred Philps and Howard Israel, to mention a few. Visitations from other pioneers , like Bill Knox and Matthew McMath, were always a treat.

The twelfth of July is an important day to Orangemen, commemorating the Battle of the Boyne in Northern Ireland, where King James was defeated by King William of Orange, to re-establish freedom of religion in the realm.

About 1960, the Orangemen decided to sell the Hall to the Mount Lehman Athletic Association, at a price that they could afford, hoping that it would be maintained as a community hall."

3. The Central Fraser Valley Fairs Association

First, a little of Dad's history of previous Fairs which were popular in our area:

> *"The pioneer settlers of the Mount Lehman area tended to show and sell their produce in the New Westminster market. The New Westminster Fair was the big event from about 1858 on. So between 1874, when Alben Hawkins arrived in Mount Lehman, and 1911, it was in that Fair that Mount Lehmaners participated. The next closest fair was Chilliwack.*
>
> *In 1910, a number of Mount Lehman Pioneers got together and decided to invite other areas of Matsqui Municipality to form an association to enhance agriculture and horticulture. So it was that the Matsqui Agricultural and Horticultural Association was formed. This organization staged the 'Gifford Fair' for many years. I entered a sample of my handwriting in the Gifford Fair in 1931, the last year of this fair. Then it amalgamated with the Poplar Group and re-formed under the name of the Central Fraser Valley Fairs Association, staging fairs in Clearbrook and Abbotsford, and then back to the Clearbrook Area. I was active in this Fair organization, being President for 6 years, and upgrading this fair organization to what is called Class 'B' status. Later I was made a life member. This fair is still held each summer.*
>
> *In, 1984 the Mount Lehman Community celebrated the 100th birthday of the school (110 years as a community), and after this successful event it was decided to organize a Mount Lehman Country Fair. It was held under the wing of the Mount Lehman Community Association, the Mount Lehman Parent-Teachers*

*Group and the Mount Lehman United Church. The first fair
was held September 20, 1986, and it was a smashing success!"*

4. Development of Merryfield Ave. Subdivision

In the early 1960s, Dad formed a partnership with Edwin Olund,
in property development. This was prior to him running for a seat
on Matsqui Council. They arranged to purchase a plot of property,
approximately 14 acres in size, and made an application to sub-
divide the property into about a dozen lots for resale. Edwin was
a builder, and he also owned a small bulldozer, and Dad handled
the paperwork to steer the application through Council. They had
to drill a water well, as at that time Mount Lehman was not ser-
viced by a municipal water system, so they located it near where the
Mount Lehman Fire Hall #5 was later situated. This provided the
water they needed. They also had to survey the lots and build a road,
which became Merryfield Avenue, a name Dad chose to honour the
pioneer Merryfield family, whose farm was located directly across
Mount Lehman Road from the new Merryfield Avenue.

This subdivision was very popular, and sold out quickly. I remember that the corner lots on Mount Lehman and Merryfield sold for
about $2,500. Dad's partner Edwin built a house on one of the lots,
as an example of what could be done, and it sold quickly as well.

5. Matsqui-Sumas-Abbotsford Minor Hockey Association

In the early 1980s my brother Doug became interested in playing
ice hockey, and Dad largely became responsible for driving Doug to
the practises or games, which often were early in the morning. Dad

would take Doug, drop him off, and curl up under a blanket in the back seat of his car to get a few more winks of sleep before he would venture out to watch Doug play.

I am not quite sure how, but he joined the executive of the MSA Minor Hockey Association, and acted as its President for a few years. This was a fledgling organization at first, because there were no hockey rinks in the MSA Area until Dad was elected to Matsqui Council, in the late 1960s. I remember that he, as Mayor, personally went to the house of the lady who owned the property on which the MSA Arena was built, and negotiated its purchase from her.

6. Red Ensign Club of Canada

In the mid-1960s, Dad became absolutely incensed that the Parliament of Canada was considering replacing his beloved Canadian Red Ensign Flag, with a maple leaf flag, that people called "Pearson's Pennant". From his point of view, all his friends, and families that he knew in Mount Lehman, were either veterans themselves, or relatives of veterans that had served Canada in many conflicts, including the Boer War, the First World War, or the Second World War, and they all fought under the Canadian Red Ensign.

Most people would express their extreme displeasure with an issue like this, decide they couldn't do anything about it anyway, and move on. Not Dad. He decided that this was an issue on which he would stand or fall! With a number of like-minded people in British Columbia, they formed a non-profit society in British Columbia, called the "Red Ensign Club of Canada, British Columbia Division". Dad became the President. They had several thousand members.

The Parliament of Canada, under then-Prime Minister Pearson, conducted a "flag" debate. John Diefenbaker, the Opposition Leader, vociferously defended the Canadian Red Ensign, but the Pearson Liberals invoked "closure" in the House of Commons, to cut off debate, and a new maple leaf Canada flag was adopted in 1965. Dad was not amused!

7. MSA Pioneers Association

The above association was formed in 1938, and each year has an annual banquet. MSA Pioneers are considered those who have lived in the MSA area for at least 40 years, and who are more than 50 years old. Each year, a few pioneers are recognized and honoured.

Mum and Dad were active members of this Association, and Dad was an executive member, and they both attended the banquets each year. Sharon and I have also attended on occasion.

8. Mount Lehman Enhancement Society

Just prior to Dad's passing, he formed a new group, with which he was actively working, to preserve the institutions of Mount Lehman (like the Post Office) and develop a Neighbourhood Plan for Mount Lehman. It would also have done more work on Mount Lehman history and genealogy, and perhaps found a permanent space for a Mount Lehman archive.

As must be apparent by now, he had a vast appetite for local history. People for miles around would come to him to track down long lost relatives, or ask questions about early Mount Lehman history, and get help to dig out documents, or help with research. The Enhancement Group was a perfect segue to his retirement years -but there was only one problem -he didn't make it to retirement.

Chapter 9

ARTWORK

"Be it long or short, rough or smooth,
We mean to reach our journey's end."

—*Churchill.*

**This is a sketch Dad drew for the Phillip
Sheffield yearbook.**

In a previous chapter, I have mentioned Dad's pen and ink sketches, drawn when in high school. Unfortunately, I do not have examples of his artwork from the RCAF newsletters. I have appended the Mount Lehman chapter of the "Where Trails Meet" booklet, mentioned earlier, as Appendix 2 . I also have sketches he drew for an early Anavets newsletter, called the "Veterans News"; I have excerpts from some 1954 and 1955 editions.

This sketch of our son Ryan was painted by Dad one day, when we were fishing at Duncan's Bar on the Fraser.

This is a water-colour painted by Dad for Sharon and me. This was Mum and Dad's view looking north from their Taylor Road house.

After Mum and Dad married, and after kids were born, Dad's pencil or brush was never that far away from his reach. His artwork was relaxing to him. He was relied upon, at birthdays, for example, to decorate each family member's birthday cakes, by creating unique designs in icing atop each cake. Then, at Hallowe'en, he would pick up a knife (as his brush equivalent) and carve most intricate designs on the front of each pumpkin, ingeniously sculpting the front of the pumpkin to allow light from the candle to be visible without cutting all the cuts right through the pumpkin - these were works of art, which we kids could not emulate.

Then there was colouring; when as young guys we were learning to colour, Dad would show us how - he amazed us kids that he could colour so well, and not go outside the lines either. He had an easel set up quite often, with a T-square, and would leave his work-in-progress out for the family to see. He would draw, or make signs, or designs - whatever struck him at the moment. He would make whole models (for example, of a new "Fraser City" design concept), and then he would model the whole project out of paper mache, which he would then put on display (for Matsqui Council, or at public meetings, for example).

I mentioned his many trips to Mexico. He had an old leather briefcase that he would bring along, containing his painting supplies. When he got to Mexico, (initially to Puerto Vallarta,) he would then take out a suitable size backing board, and tape his drawing paper to it, and then start painting. Sometimes, he would draw practise sketches on small scratch pads, and then transfer those ideas to the bigger canvas. I remember at least one year in Mexico in which he held art classes for Karen and Ryan, quite anxious that they try their hands at water-colours, painting hibiscus flowers.

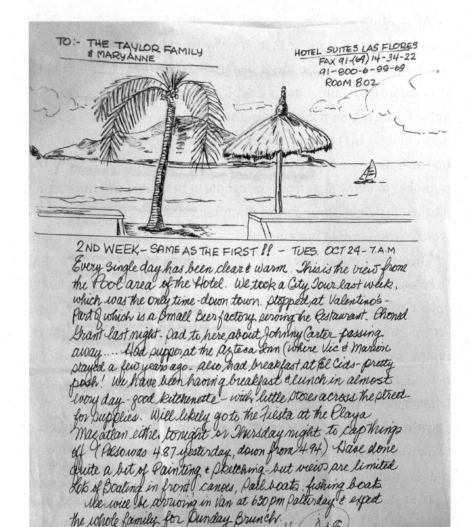

TO :- THE TAYLOR FAMILY & MARYANNE

HOTEL SUITES LAS FLORES
FAX 91-(69) 14-34-22
91-800-6-99-69
ROOM 802

2ND WEEK - SAME AS THE FIRST !! - TUES. OCT 24 - 7. A.M
Every single day has been clear & warm. This is the view from
the Pool area of the Hotel. We took a City Tour last week,
which was the only time - down town. Stopped at Valentino's -
Part of which is a small Beer factory, serving the Restaurant. Phoned
Grant last night - Dad to, here about Johnny Carter passing
away..... Had supper at the Azteca Inn (where Vic & Marion
stayed a few years ago - also, had breakfast at El Cids - pretty
posh! We have been having breakfast & lunch in almost
every day - good kitchenette - with little stores across the street -
for supplies. Will likely go to the Fiesta at the Playa
Mazatlan either tonight or Thursday night to cap things
off (Pesos was 4.87 yesterday, down from 4.94) Have done
quite a bit of Painting & Sketching - but views are limited
Lots of Boating in front canoes, sail boats, fishing boats
We will be arriving in Van at 6:30 pm Saturday & expect
the whole family for Sunday Brunch.
Hope things have been going well!! (G&G)

Before the age of computers, email, texts, etc, Dad would fax us folks back home
while they were in Mexico. They enjoyed something like 71 trips there over the
years. The above is the type of chatty fax he would send.

Dad's last painting done in Mexico in early 1998. (He died on February 22, 1998)

A water-colour of a winter scene with skiers, painted by Dad for my brother Grant and his wife Carol.

When Mum and Dad first went to San Jose del Cabo, they stayed at La Jolla condominiums. Dad did a lot of drawing and painting there, as all the sights in Los Cabos were new to him. An art show was held each year in the beautiful lobby of the La Jolla complex, and at least on one occasion, Dad was invited to display his art work at a table, to show off his work and and see all other artists' work. A series of his Mexican beach paintings are displayed in our Unit 44 condo in San Jose del Cabo.

Another of Dad's sketches to depict a story of how goods were transported by river in the early days.(Where Trails Meet)

Continuing with the artistic theme, Dad was also interested in poetry; I remember many evenings spent at the Army and Navy Club in Mount Lehman, listening to Dad and Len Philps reciting their favourite poems. One of Dad's favourites was the following poem by Barry Cornwall, the first stanza of which follows:

The Sea

The Sea! the sea! the open sea!
The blue, the fresh, the ever free!
Without a mark, without a bound,
It runneth the earth's wide regions round;
It plays with the clouds; it mocks the skies;
Or like a cradled creature lies.

Appendix 2 to this book is the chapter of the book "Where Trails Meet", about Mount Lehman, which Dad penned in 1958. He really was a man of many talents!

A Century-Sam type character also graced the pages of Where Trails Meet.

Dad contributed to a 1958 booklet called "Where Trails Meet", which told the story of the communities making up Matsqui, Sumas and Abbotsford at that time. This sketch by Dad evidenced the importance of the railway in the Central Fraser Valley.

Dad drew this sketch for Where Trails Meet to show Matsqui Dike- building.

Dad drew this cartoon in 1974, as a satirical comment on political issues of the day, during his time as Mayor of Matsqui.

Chapter 10

POLITICAL INTEREST DOWN THROUGH THE YEARS

Dad had an immense interest in politics, mostly, but not exclusively, in Canada. To narrow down his interests within Canada, I will divide them into three broad categories:

1. Provincial Politics in British Columbia

In a previous chapter, I quoted from Dad's notes, from when he was a teenager. This is when his interest in Provincial politics was piqued, due to his father's influence. The family had always supported the Conservative party, but strange things started to happen in British Columbia, in the late 1940s. The Provincial Conservative leader, Herb Anscomb, was challenged by an upstart politician from Kelowna, named WAC Bennett, [later known colloquially as 'Wacky Bennett'.] Bennett started out his political life as a Conservative, but he lost the leadership challenge to Herb Anscomb; he then affiliated himself with the Social Credit movement, which originated in Alberta. In the early 1950s, Bennett won his first Provincial election in BC under the Social Credit banner. Dad and his father did not appreciate Bennett's intrusion into the Provincial scene, and his ouster of the Conservatives in the election.

Everyone in BC thought Bennett's win was a "flash in the pan", not the least the Provincial Conservative movement. This is, no doubt, the reason for Dad's father, (Buster's) run to be elected in 1954, and Dad's subsequent two unsuccessful local riding challenges to the Socreds, running against Chilliwack MLA Ken Kiernan, in the Provincial elections of 1956 and 1960. But, alas, the Socreds were not to be a temporary aberration in BC politics, being returned again and again to form government. In effect, the Socreds were a coalition of most of the mainstream Liberals and Conservatives (not unlike the current Liberal Party in BC). However, Dad was not amongst the throng. He thought that the Socreds had some unconventional ideas, from fiscal and other standpoints. However, he voted for the Socreds, when there was no Conservative candidate on the ballot, to keep out the NDP. His distrust of the Socreds, though, did not abate, and always simmered just below the surface. He took one more crack at defeating the local MLA and Cabinet Minister, Robert McLellan, in our local riding, under the Provincial Conservative banner once again, but was once again defeated, in 1973. Dad never ran again for Provincial Office. His principles mattered to him, above all else. He was against big government, and big business controlling who got elected. He refused to accept donations except from individual voters, eschewing corporate sponsorships and contributions.

2. Federal Canadian Politics

I alluded to Dad's interest in the Canadian Federal political scene in a previous chapter - attending at the Parliament Buildings in Ottawa several times during his active service in the RCAF. Later, when he returned to Mount Lehman, he became active in the federal Conservative party. To quote from Dad's notes, under the heading of "First Political Trip to the Capital" he says:

"The Nation's capital, Ottawa, is a thrilling city to visit. During the war, I visited it a number of times, you might say, as a 'service tourist.' But in 1948, I was elected to attend the annual meeting of the Progressive Conservative party of Canada, as a "Young Conservative" delegate. Two Young Conservatives from British Columbia were given this opportunity by the Party - the President of the Young Conservatives of BC and myself, a Vice-President. Since I had just married a year previously, my wife Elsie and I arranged our meagre finances so that with a basket full of sandwiches and goodies, and a careful budget, the trip was made possible. What a wonderful opportunity it was to participate in the deliberations of this great national Party!

I was on the organization committee, under the chairmanship of Leon Balcer, MP, a budding young French Canadian, who later became National President of the Young Conservatives, and a Cabinet Minister during the first Diefenbaker government. Here we were, entertained by General George Pearkes VC; I met Donald Fleming MP and heard John Diefenbaker in action for the first time. It was at this meeting that many of us decided that new leadership was emerging in Canada. A new vigorous leader of pioneer Western action. We did not know that it would take eight years before we were able to receive this leadership of John Diefenbaker. But we did know that he truly spoke for those of us who knew that the Progressive Conservative party would save Canada from reactionary programmes and that progress and social justice must emerge together.

Such was this brief visit to the Nation's Capital, being only three days, but what a thrilling experience for a Young Conservative. Since that time the Party has increased representation from youth organizations to the degree that almost one-third of the delegates today are from ages 18-35. If a Party intends to remain the party of the future it is essential that this trend remains."

Dad was so impressed by his experience with the federal Conservatives, especially at the 1948 Convention, that he continued to work diligently within the local federal constituency association thereafter. When John Diefenbaker became the leader of the party, Dad let his name stand at the nominating convention to elect candidates for the 1957 Federal election, in the Fraser Valley constituency. He ran in that convention against Harold Hicks, and he lost the nomination race by 3 votes. Thereafter, Harold Hicks, became one of the members of parliament elected in the Diefenbaker election victory. A few more votes at the nominating meeting, and Dad would have been the MP for Fraser Valley in 1957, who surely would have been re-elected in the Diefenbaker sweep of 1958!

My experience in 1967 followed Dad's in 1957 - I was a youth voting delegate in 1967 to the Progressive Conservative Party Leadership Convention in Maple Leaf Gardens in Toronto. Dad was a regular delegate. It was such an honour to be able to travel to Toronto and attend as a delegate, with Dad, at that convention. What an experience to be a part of the process of electing the next leader of our Party. But, as had happened a few times before, we picked the wrong horse. We supported Dief the Chief to continue as leader, but when he was knocked off the ballot, we then switched our loyalties to Duff Roblin (the Premier of Manitoba at the time). The result of the ballot, no thanks to Dad or me, is history - Robert Stanfield became the new leader of the Progressive Conservative Party of Canada.

Dad's Federal and Provincial aspirations were put on hold, due to events which occurred in 1966 - details on this next.

My brother Grant, meeting Prime Minister Diefenbaker with Dad, during a 1958 campaign rally.

3. Matsqui Municipal Political Interest

By 1966, Dad had been a member of the various iterations of the Conservative party for 24 years. His political experience made him one of the most senior politicians in the Central Fraser Valley to have never been elected to office. If he had been a professor at a university, he could have taught Political Science, with all his experience! But as I have noted throughout this book, he was rather busy with his businesses, his family and all the other activities in the community that I have detailed. His family wrongly thought that he had no more time for politics!

Matsqui Council, with Dad as Councillor. In the back row from L to R -Dad, Andy Jackman, Bill Scott and Harold Janzen. Front row: Gordon Gardner, Spud Murphy (Reeve) and Jim McDonald.

TO THE VOTERS OF MATSQUI

In the 6 months that I have served on Matsqui Council since the By-Election I have conscientiously worked with the council team and at the same time have introduced what I believe are constructive views.

★ I have urged council to set up a parks committee to plan future civic properties.

★ I believe that recreation for young and old is one of the area's most pressing problems. A renewed effort should be made for a recreation arena for MSA, a good project to initiate under the new "Regional District" proposal.

★ I support the council for a "YES VOTE" on the Hospital By-Law.

I have enjoyed this work and am earnestly seeking your support for a full two year term.

I would ask that you consider the above, as well as my Fair Board work, Zoning Board chairmanship, and my interest in public affairs for many years.
— Doug Taylor

On Dec. 10, For Matsqui Council, Re-elect
TAYLOR, Douglas   X

This is the ad Dad placed in the local newspaper in December of 1966 after he had fulfilled his term in the by-election to succeed his father on Council

But sometimes opportunity knocks quietly. In his case, after his father had been ill with colon cancer for two years, he passed away, in 1966. At the time, his father, H.E. (Buster) Taylor was a sitting member of the council of the Municipality of Matsqui. As a result of his death, a by-election was required to fill the position, and Dad decided to throw his hat into the ring. The Councillor position was only for a six month term, until the regular municipal election, but Dad filed his papers and was successful in being elected.

Dad served the 6-month term as Councillor (as the position was then called, soon changing to Alderman), and then, in December of 1966, he ran again for a two-year term.

Once again, he was elected, in this case, topping the poll. So it was that Dad's municipal career was launched, which spanned many years. Of course, Dad's father would have discussed with him, over the years, all the issues involved in being a Matsqui Councillor; Dad was a quick learner, as he just loved political life!

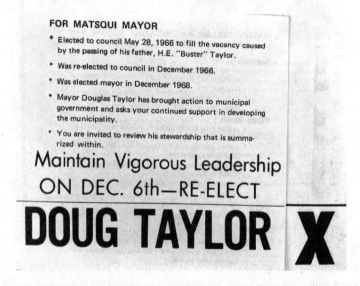

FOR MATSQUI MAYOR

* Elected to council May 28, 1966 to fill the vacancy caused by the passing of his father, H.E. "Buster" Taylor.

* Was re-elected to council in December 1966.

* Was elected mayor in December 1968.

* Mayor Douglas Taylor has brought action to municipal government and asks your continued support in developing the municipality.

* You are invited to review his stewardship that is summarized within.

Maintain Vigorous Leadership
ON DEC. 6th—RE-ELECT
DOUG TAYLOR X

This is the brochure our church Hi-C group, including my future wife Sharon, helped hand out throughout the Municipality.

Dad would serve only 1 year of his 2-year term as Councillor, before deciding to let his name stand as Reeve. In the meantime, he immersed himself in his new role, as Alderman.

Matsqui consisted of a huge area, stretching from Aldergrove to McCallum Road, and including all of Matsqui Prairie, its north boundary being the Fraser River, and its south boundary being the US border. Matsqui's population, at that time, was well below

20,000. By comparison, the municipalities to the east, namely Abbotsford and Sumas, had populations of approximately 1,000 and 5,000 respectively.

Prior to Dad's term of office, the position of Reeve (soon to change to the term Mayor during Dad's term) was a part-time position, as were the Councillors' positions. When Dad studied the situation, he realized that the municipality's governance had to become much more businesslike to accommodate future growth in the area. Dad was the first Matsqui Mayor to establish regular office hours, and appointment access to the Mayor, as he could see that the Mayor and Council needed to take a far more active role in decision-making. He just loved municipal politics, and there was no job too big or too small for him. One day he would be greeting Queen Elizabeth, or installing the Royal Westminster Regiment with the Freedom of the Municipality; the next day he would be out checking a taxpayer's flooded basement, later stopping to work at his insurance office, and then, when he got home, feeding his cattle.

The whole Central Fraser Valley area was called the "MSA" area, for Matsqui, Sumas and Abbotsford, and Dad also could see that more cooperation was needed on issues which affected the whole area. The biggest issue facing the MSA area when Dad was elected to Council was that there were no ice-hockey facilities, unlike all the surrounding municipalities. Worse than that, successive referenda had been voted on by all three local municipalities, and Matsqui was the lone holdout in not approving the building of an arena. He felt it had to be a priority to get this project built.

When Dad was 43 years old, he entered the electoral contest to become Matsqui's Mayor. The incumbent, J.A. (Spud) Murphy, had been Mayor for 6 years, and was a high school classmate at Philip Sheffield High. Dad's campaign was low budget; he made his own election signs and put them up, with family help. No-one had a lot of money in those days to lavish on fancy signage, or radio ads. I remember helping him put up signs at the most prominent intersections around the municipality (for this election, and others). Then he had some brochures printed - a nice compact size that could be handed out, or could be placed on car windshields. Sharon and I, and many of our friends from our United Church youth group, helped place brochures on car windshields.

Douglas Taylor, incumbent Matsqui councillor, kept a lead in the race for the reeve's seat in the municipality following a recount Wednesday. Mr. Taylor, leading by 19 votes over Reeve J. A. (Spud) Murphy, had his margin cut to 13 when the recount was completed around 7 p.m. Wednesday night. Unless a judicial recount is called, Mr. Taylor has been elected and will serve as reeve for the next two years. He is shown here with his wife Elsie after learning he had defeated Mr. Murphy.   (Brian McCristall photo)

Mum and Dad at Matsqui Municipal Hall the night of the first mayoralty election - after a recount, Dad won by 13 votes!

As The Valley Tribune reported, on December 13, 1967, "*Douglas Taylor has unofficially become the new Reeve of Matsqui in one of the most closely and hotly contested elections ever held in the municipality.*"

On election night, it was announced that Dad had a 19-vote lead over Murphy. Because of the closeness in votes, a recount was called for the next day, and Dad was officially declared the winner, by 13 votes. Unfortunately, the civic centre referendum in Matsqui only passed by a vote of 52%, whereas 60% was required to go ahead with the project.

A 1975 Matsqui Council meeting, with Dad presiding as Mayor. Council members are Spud Murphy, Bob Brady, Harry de Jong, Dad, Ray Kirkwood, Chuck Wiebe and Jim McDonald.

So the task of governing the District of Matsqui, over the next 8 years, fell to Dad and his Council. There was some friction on Council, over the years, as there always is, but a majority of the members of Council usually worked together to achieve common objectives. Dad truly was a visionary in his views. He had the ability to look to the future planning of the municipality, and to determine what the needs would be many years out.

I will mention one of the significant issues of the day, namely the location of large shopping centres. The Mayor of Sumas, George Ferguson, favoured locating the shopping area in the Sumas Way area, which was located in the District of Sumas Municipality. Dad favoured locating the shopping centres, and other businesses, on South Fraser Way, between Clearbrook townsite and downtown Abbotsford. This became a political football for several years. Luckily, Dad stuck to his guns and managed to entice Grosvenor International to locate Sevenoaks Shopping Centre where Dad advocated; to do otherwise he felt would have changed the whole shopping complexion of the MSA area. In hindsight, this was a brilliant decision. The shopping district in the present City has now stretched from Abbotsford to Clearbrook, with a present City population of about 150,000.

Dad, centre, with Aldermen Bill Scott, on left, and Andy Jackman.

I list some of the major accomplishments and highlights of his administration:

- The passing of the civic centre referendum, and the building in Matsqui of a state of the art ice-hockey facility (operated jointly by the 3 municipalities;)

- the previously mentioned building of Sevenoaks Shopping Centre, by Grosvenor International, thereby establishing the largest shopping facility in the Central Fraser Valley, in the Clearbrook-Abbotsford corridor; see the photo attached as Chapter 10, Endnote 7, of Mum making the first purchase at Eaton's on opening day;

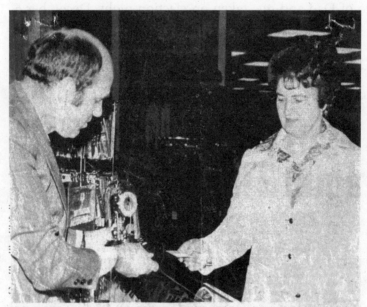

1　Ross Belsher, store manager of Eaton's Sevenoaks greets the first official customer opening day, Mrs. Elsie Taylor, wife of Mayor Douglas Taylor of Matsqui, who officially opened the centre October 15.

Mum was the first customer at Eaton's Sevenoaks, on opening day. Ross Belcher, the store manager, later became the Member of Parliament for the Fraser Valley riding.

- the installation of a municipal-wide water system;
- the establishment of Mount Lehman Fire Hall #5, and Mount Lehman Library;
- the building of a new courthouse, Crown Counsel office, and Matsqui Police facility;
- upgrading of Municipal Hall, and Municipal Works Yard facilities;
- establishment and upgrading of rim road corridors, to plan for the traffic of the future - examples are MacClure Road and Downes Road;

Dad was re-elected as Mayor in 1969, 1971 and 1973. I attach a photo of Dad and me, taken on election night, December 6, 1969, with the election poll results in the background.

This photo is of Dad (Mayor of Matsqui), on left, George Ferguson (Mayor of Sumas), centre, and Peter Crocker (Mayor of Abbotsford), early 1970s.

Dad was defeated in the Mayoral election of 1975, by Harry de Jong, but notwithstanding that defeat, he ran again for council, and was elected for two terms as Alderman in Matsqui - from 1977 to 1978, and again from 1980 to 1981.

Here I am with with my Dad at the Municipal Hall on election night, 1969.

A fitting tribute to Dad's work on Matsqui Council was penned by Kurt Langmann, the editor of the Aldergrove Star newspaper, after Dad's death in February, 1998. I quote from it in part: The heading was "Highly regarded man laid to his rest":

"Doug's accomplishments are so numerous, it's hard to find a starting point, but his earnest intelligence and his graciousness were the keys to his high regard among all those who knew

him. Even among those who challenged him politically, and sometimes beat him in competition, there was always respect for the little man with big ideas.

I first came to know Doug well, when I started at The Star in 1973, assigned to report on Matsqui Council when Doug was Mayor. He was on council for 14 years, eight as Mayor. In many ways I was inspired by his example of community activism, and learned much from him about how to get a job done. He felt strongly that the rural areas of western Matsqui and eastern Langley Township were shortchanged by the more urban power centres of the two districts, and while his dream of a new municipality was quashed by the march of time and amalgamation, he left a lasting legacy in the form of municipal water service to most of the far flung areas of the former Matsqui.

When I would drive out to visit Doug at his Mount Lehman insurance office, I couldn't help but notice that the community had fire hydrants. Back in the days when municipalities only had to pay one-quarter of the cost of water service, and senior governments paid the rest, he still had to fight a reluctant council to get this basic infrastructure investment approved. He would shake his head at the 'tunnel vision' of his counterparts in Langley Township, who altogether refused to bring municipal water to the south and east sides of the Township. …Doug's eldest son, Gordon gave an outstanding eulogy to his father at the service, in the company of Doug's mother Dorothy, wife Elsie, brother Jim, children Gordon, Grant, Rosemary and Doug Jr. Gordon noted the irony that Doug passed away the same day the Winter Olympics came to an end: 'You could say that Dad's life was a lot like the Olympics ... his life could really have been called the Mount Lehman Olympics."

The Abbotsford newspaper's article, reporting on Dad's death, contained the headline "Gold Medal Mayor Mourned", also a reference to my remarks in the eulogy which I gave at Dad's service.

Several honours were bestowed upon Dad, after his service on council and to the community. First he was given the honour of Freeman of the District of Matsqui, in 1988, and later two posthumous awards: the "Order of Abbotsford", (as the amalgamation of the three districts occurred in 1995), and in a permanent tribute, in 2004, then Mayor Mary Reeves (on behalf of the City of Abbotsford) dedicated a park to his name, which is called "Douglas Taylor Park", located on Harris Road (not far from the Taylor farm). At the ribbon-cutting ceremony for the dedication of the park, I spoke and thanked the city and council for the honour bestowed on Dad.

A complete copy of the eulogy which I gave at his service, on February 27, 1998, at Mount Lehman Church, is attached as Appendix 6 .

Chapter 11

REFLECTIONS

I hope you have enjoyed this story. It's not just the story of Dad's life, but necessarily, the story of the Taylor family. It may not be the story as Dad would have told it. I am not entirely sure how his book (or books) would have gone, as he left so many notes, on various topics. I know for sure he would have emphasized the Mount Lehman pioneer families more than I have, but there were so few of them left when I came on the scene that I never got to meet or know most of them. So I could only give you a taste of the stories of these men and women who settled our little village, albeit written by Dad's hand.

Dad's notes on his political thoughts were extensive - I am sure he wanted to write on these topics in detail. When he was involved in Provincial politics, and ran in our riding for the Progressive Conservatives, he was particularly interested in topics concerning agriculture. He understood the problems which farmers had, and actually wrote agriculture policy that he thought should be adopted Provincially. This also applied to other areas as well. He wanted to be a part of a political party where he could develop policy, not just follow policies developed by others. I believe this philosophy was what made him successful in municipal politics as well.

Dad's interest in his family's genealogy was not understood by me until later in my life. I understand it now, however. If I would have taken an interest earlier, I would have paid far more attention to what he was saying. It would have been so easy for me to express more interest in the topics he mentioned, and flesh them out while I could. It would have made my job writing this book much easier. As it is, everything had to be researched extensively by me before being relied upon. The impetus for me finally getting interested in family genealogy was when I met our cousins in Nova Scotia, in 1997, at a reunion of the Taylor family, most of which branches had not gotten together for over one hundred years. I could then see the bigger picture, that Dad had seen all along. Understanding the ancestry of our family enabled me to see that it wasn't just tracing our ancestors down through the years that was important, but understanding how and why they evolved as they did; for example, why their beliefs in the British Crown were so strong that they would leave their new homeland (in the United States) after having lived there for almost 150 years, and also why they would leave the Province of Nova Scotia, and move to British Columbia, in 1887. Dad and I had to have answers to these questions!

Dad also wrote extensively on the subject of the history of the Matsqui area, including Mount Lehman. I can't tell if those writings were intended to be a separate book, or simply a chapter in a more over-arching story. In any event, I borrowed heavily from his thoughts in each of the areas of his writing, to give an idea of his thoughts that would have translated into his own book, had he lived longer than his 73 years.

In 1998, Dad passed the torch to his family, and we have carried on. This task, without his guidance, has been made easier (but not easy), by the strength of character he exemplified, and all the things he taught us.

I have written this family story in hopes that my children, grand-children, (and other family members), and future generations, will gain some insight into the lives of their ancestors. I hope they find answers to their questions about their heritage and I challenge them to continue the saga, ask questions while they can, and write their own stories sooner rather than later.

Reference Materials

Chapter One

1. Family research notes of Douglas Grant Burton Taylor, Marlean Rhodenizer, Pat Rhodenizer, Debbie Zwicker and Gordon Taylor, as a result of research conducted over many years.

2. Research on ancestry.com as to the Taylor family.

3. Nova Scotia census records.

4. City of New Westminster web site and notes re dedication of heritage sites.

5. Land Title Office records, New Westminster, BC.

6. Census of Canada records, 1881-1910.

7. Letters, notes and documents left by Burton and Anna Taylor and their families, found in Dad's records.

8. BC Directories, found in the New Westminster Archives, and online, 1889-1910.

9. Wigwams to Windmills, 1977, Ridgedale Women's Institute, and especially the portion written by Bill Lancaster.

10. Olivet Baptist Church records, New Westminster, BC.

11. Chute Family in America, Wm Chute, 1894.

12. Nooksack Tales and Trails, PR Jeffcott, 1949.

13. The Langley Story, 1977, Donald Waite.

14. Royal Engineers BC website.

15. Nova Scotia Archives, Halifax, NS.

16. Where Trails Meet, 1958, MSA Centennial Society.

17. Mount Lehman United Church archival records, Mount Lehman BC.

18. Notes, photos and other materials loaned to me by Donna Kingman, Brian Kingman, and Janet Andris, including their publication "Taylor Family of Mount Lehman", written in 2005.

Chapter 2

1. Notes made by Dad during his lifetime.

2. Province of BC Archives, Victoria, BC, especially the diary of Alben Hawkins.

3. Royal Engineers BC website.

4. Farm Museum, Fort Langley, BC, displays of the settlement of the Fraser Valley.

5. The Vintage Car Magazine, published by the Vintage Car Club of Canada, BC.

6. The Mount Lehman Chapter in the book Where Trails Meet, written by Dad.

7. Web research re the Canadian National Railway.

Chapter 3

1. Notes written by James Edward Norton Taylor.

2. Photographs, letters and documents loaned to me by Donna Kingman and Janet Andris.

3. The Reach Gallery, Abbotsford, BC, and especially property tax records of the District of Matsqui.

4. Notes of Gordon Bretelle as to various Taylor family members.

5. The Place Between, Alder Grove Heritage Society, 1993.

6. Abbotsford, Sumas and Matsqui Newspaper, 1951 article by EK Wilson.

7. Interview notes of my interview with my grandmother, Dorothy Elizabeth Forrester Taylor, about 1988.

8. Notes, records and documents of my great-grandfather, James Grant Forrester.

9. Gordon Bretelle's notes.

Chapter 4

1. Notes made after my interview with Dorothy Elizabeth Forrester Taylor.

2. Dad's notes re the Forrester families.

3. Forrester bookkeeping and tax and other records, found by me in a pump-house at Mum and Dad's house.

4. James Forrester's records re his occupation as a Law Agent in Scotland.

5. Letters and notes of James Grant Forrester detailing the events surrounding the family leaving Scotland.

6. Research notes of Ian Smith LL B., former Land Titles Registrar, New Westminster Land Title Office, done at my request (2021), as to White Rock lot. (Ian was also my classmate at UBC Law School)

Chapter 5

1. The Place Between, 1993, and especially an article written by James Edward Norton Taylor.

2. Heart of the Fraser Valley, Loretta Riggins and Len Walker, 1991.

3. School yearbooks of Philip Sheffield High School, 1940-1943.

4. Dad's notes entitled "A Quarter Century in the Front Line", re his political perspective, and other notes on Canadian politics.

Chapter 6

1. Dad's notes re RCAF service.

2. History of Hall #5, Mount Lehman Fire Department, given to me by Brian Denny of Mount Lehman.

Chapter 7

1. Dad's notes re returning to Mount Lehman after WWII, and how he started his businesses.

2.   Walls With Strong Foundations, Ben Wall, 1992.

3.   James and Elizabeth Forrester's notes and records.

Chapter 8

1.   Dad's notes re the history of Unit 315, Army and Navy Veterans in Canada.

2.   Notes of James Edward Norton Taylor re the building of the Mount Lehman cenotaph.

3.   Dad's notes re Loyal Orange Lodge #1868.

4.   Dad's notes re the history of Central Fraser Valley Fairs and Exhibitions.

5.   Dad's notes re the Merryfield Ave, Mount Lehman subdivision.

6.   Dad's notes re the Red Ensign Club of Canada.

Chapter 9

1.   Philip Sheffield High School yearbooks, 1940-1943.

Chapter 10

1.   Dad's notes re his political interests.

2.   Various articles and publications in the Abbotsford, Sumas and Matsqui Newspaper.

Appendices

1. Confusion Resolved over how Mount Lehman
    School was Established

2. Where Trails Meet - Chapter on Mount Lehman

3. The Story of Mount Lehman Church

4. History of Mount Lehman Library

5. History of Matsqui Unit 315 - Army, Navy and Air
    Force Veterans in Canada

6. Eulogy for Douglas Grant Burton Taylor at his
    funeral Service on February 27, 1998

Appendix 1

CONFUSION RESOLVED OVER HOW MOUNT LEHMAN SCHOOL WAS ESTABLISHED

By Gordon Taylor, 2015

For some years there has been confusion over exactly what occurred at the time of the establishment of Mount Lehman's School. Taylor family relatives told us that James Bangs, Anna Taylor's cousin, donated a portion of the property he owned and the school was established in 1884. A contrary view, raised by the Israel family of Mount Lehman, was that an Israel ancestor, John Israel, donated the land.

In 2015, I attended at the New Westminster Land Title Office to verify the establishment of the school by examining the actual title documents. First, I searched the title to the property now owned by the Taylors, but which was acquired by James Bangs. That parcel was originally given as a Crown Grant to Isaac Lehman, in 1878. In 1882, Lehman sold the property to George Bellrose. In the same year, Bellrose transferred the property to our relative, James Bangs. We know that the school opened at the corner of Taylor and Mount Lehman Road in 1884, while Mr. Bangs owned the property.

In June, 1887, Bangs transferred the property to our great-grand-mother, Anna Taylor, who had moved out from Nova Scotia that year with her entire family. After 1887, Anna Taylor transferred the eastern portion of her property to J. G. Kirks in 1891. That property changed hands again as follows:

To Annandale Duncan Grieve in 1893;

To Robert Law in 1894;

Then Robert Law transferred the property to John Israel in 1901. So after the school was established in 1884, the property on which the school was situated was owned by Bangs, Anna Taylor, Kirks, Grieve, Law and Israel. It was finally transferred to the Matsqui School Board by John Israel in 1916.

The above information required explanation to make sense to me. If our relative Bangs donated the school property for school pur-poses in 1884, why did the School Board only get title to the land in 1916? Fortunately, I solved this mystery by the chance finding of certain articles in a newspaper called the "Abbotsford Post", in the year 1910. (The newspaper was found online, in the University of British Columbia collection.) An article in the May 6, 1910 edition, under the heading "Matsqui School Board Meets", states in part:

"A regular meeting of the Matsqui School Board was held in the Municipal Hall on Saturday, April 23rd, at 3 p.m., with Trustees Cruikshanks (Chairman), Conroy, McPhee, Merryfield and Ross being present. ...Re Mt. Lehman School, informing the Board that a school would be erected this place as soon as a copy of the deed for a new site was forwarded for inspection, as the present site did not either belong to the Board or Government. The board at this time was not prepared to take up the matter of a new site, as this would be best arranged at a later meeting, but at the same time would make a protest if the present site could not be held after being deeded for twenty-six years and occupied all the time for school purposes. During the day a delegation from Mt. Lehman waited on the board and urged that the new school be built on the old site. The chairman, on behalf of the board, informed the delegates that a meeting would be held at Mt. Lehman on Monday afternoon, April 25th, when all matters in regard to this school could be discussed and hoped that as many of the trustees would be present as possible."

On the same page of the paper that day, another caption entitled "Mt. Lehman Meeting" says:

"The Matsqui School Board met the people of Mount Lehman on Saturday, the 23rd inst. to consider matters in connection with a new school which is very much needed in that district. The people are unanimously in favour of having the new school built on the old grounds, but there appears to have been some laxity on the part of the officials at some time as the deed of this property, which was bought and paid for by the early pioneers of Mount Lehman, had never been registered, and now the Government refuses to build a new building on land of which they have no registered title, and the people cannot see how they should be held responsible for what was certainly remissness on the part of the officials of the educational department of that day. The School Board passed a resolution asking the Government to look into the matter and endeavour if possible to have the matter rectified, and they are now awaiting developments."

It would be six more years before the school property was transferred to the Matsqui School Board by the then owner of the parcel of land, John Israel.

It was only by the persistence of the people of Mount Lehman that the present school site was saved. Those early pioneers recognized and remembered the community efforts made by James Bangs, in donating the land and giving a signed deed to the School Board in 1884, (even though it was not registered as he anticipated) and the other members of the community who no doubt cleared the land and erected the first school on the site. Thanks also to John Israel for recognizing the importance of the school in the community, and transferring the portion of his land in 1916. The community of Mount Lehman was not about to abandon this site and start again elsewhere.

Appendix 2

WHERE TRAILS MEET -
MOUNTLEHMAN CHAPTER

Mt. Lehman

Passing Fort Langley and approaching Glen Valley, travelling East up the Fraser, a heavily wooded plateau rose high against the Southern sky, an impressive challenge, for it appeared to be densely covered with mighty fir, cedar, hemlock and maple trees, with alder and birch scattered throughout. Only surveyors of the Royal Engineers had been on top of this plateau and had placed only as many markers as would meet minimum standards. Here were 10,000 acres of forest — no cleared land at all at Glen Valley, in the North-West corner of what is now Matsqui Prairie, settlers were beginning to move to the mountain's edge.

The reason that the area around Mt. Lehman was one of the first settled was naturally due to the fact that it was on high ground and safe from yearly floods. There are many disputes over who was the first settler but all are agreed that Albin Hawkins was the first to take up permanent residence about 1874, settling on the Matsqui side and including both lowland and hillside. Alf Hawkins, Mrs. Lehman assisting, was born there in 1879 and still lives in Aldergrove.

On top of the plateau there were some Indian trails used only when flooding made Matsqui Prairie impassable. No one had yet attempted to create a home in this wilderness of the great "inbetween," which covered the six miles from Glen Valley to Matsqui Prairie. The Lehman families arrived around 1879 and the river landing became known as Lehman's Landing. At a meeting a few years later, held at the Hawkin's house, a suggestion that the district be called Mt. Albin was turned down by Mr. Hawkins in favor of Mt. Lehman.

In the Spring of 1875 a river boat nosed into the cove below the mountainside and deposited Isaac Lehman on the bank. He took his long squirrel rifle and an axe, and, carrying food and clothing, climbed resolutely up through the timber at the mouth of a little stream. In this lovely forest he was the first real pioneer, for in his chosen land he had the gigantic task of hewing a path for civilization to follow; but in May and June the white blossoms of the dogwoods line the banks of the little streams and the forest casts its wondrful spell on all who enter. A year or so later Sam Lehman followed, as did Bellrose, Rogers and Bangs, and landings along the river became busy places, Marsh's, Nicholson's, Gillis', Lehman's and Burgess' Landings being frequent stops.

Joseph Patterson first arrived in the Glen Valley district in 1861, and staked his claim, but did not settl

still operates part of the original homestead. William Marsh came from Ontario to Jubilee district in 1881 and worked on the C.P.R. construction. His son Clarence still farms his homestead. P. W. McCormick located in 1881. He also worked on the C.P.R. and his son William and daughter Mary today live on the farm. The Merryfield family arrived from California in the same year, coming originally from Cornwall, England. Mr. Merryfield had passed through earlier and made preliminary plans for staking a piece of land. However, at Lehman's Landing he met a George McCallum to whom he gave all the papers and then on returning had to get another piece of land. Lee, Ross and Burgess were also new arrivals.

S.S. Skeena, the last river steamer to serve the
Fraser Valley

Neil Craig came from Ontario in 1882. He was mail carrier by rowboat from Mission to

53

Page 53, Where Trails Meet

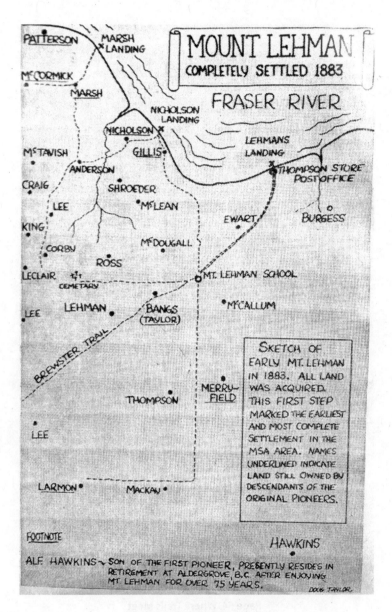

Page 52, Where Trails Meet

Mt. Lehman Post Office, the first post office service in this area. Several settlers came from Prince Edward Island. Dan Nicholson arrived in 1882. He was a harness maker. His son Danny is now President of the Fraser Valley Milk Producers' Association and a well known sports enthusiast. Grandson Danny lives on the original farm. Capt. Alex Gillis came by way of the Panama, also in 1882, and by the river boat "Enterprise," to Lehman's Landing. His son Hugh and daughter May are still our neighbors. D. B. McDougald arrived to mine gold and stayed to farm. Ed Thompson started the first store in 1883. For a while Mr. Sutherland operated a second store and Henry Alder bought out Ed. Thompson, operating the store for many years. Burton Taylor came from Nova Scotia in 1886 to a homestead owned by Mrs. Taylor's cousin, Jim Bangs. Little is known of the Bangs except that Mr. Bangs was a Royal Engineer and acquired the crown grant in 1863. Mr. H. E. Taylor owns the original homestead.   *1882.*

In the Spring of 1886 Robert Coghlan, his wife and sons, Lawrence and Charles, settled in Mt. Lehman, arriving from Fort Langley.

A third son, Frank, was born later. Charles and Lawrence became river men and few old timers will ever forget Capt. Charles, who spent his whole lifetime on Fraser and Yukon River boats. Lawrence married Catherine West whose father operated the mill on the Sumas River which cut the planks for the Sward dyke. Several Mt. Lehman families trace their relationships to the Wests.

L. Coghlan and team during contsruction of Gibson's Hall on Mt. Lehman Road, 1911

Burton and Anna Taylor, with sons John, Herbert, and Edward, arrived in 1887 at the original place left to Mrs. Taylor by her cousin, James Bangs, who had died as a result of a surveying accident. Burton Taylor was a ship's carpenter and, while the boys proceeded to clear land between periods of working in New Westminster, met Harry West and they decided to build river boats. West had acquired the Fairy Queen and with Taylor's help built many boats for himself and others. The Pheasant and the Defender operated for West on the Harrison River and were later chartered for towing logs. The Defender, skippered by Jack West, on her trip over Matsqui Prairie, picking up the cattle at the big flood time, docked at Nicholas Station near Abbotsford, and for the May 24th celebration in 1902, brought the Chilliwack band to Sumas. Ed Taylor was purser on this boat and later married Elizabeth West. Sons H. E. (Buster) and Gordon still own the original Mt. Lehman property.

Page 54, Where Trails Meet

Raising Flagpole at the First Mt. Lehman School

The MacLean brothers, Angus and John, came from Prince Edward Island in 1887. Angus farmed while John taught school. John became Minister of Education and later Premier of B.C. John Israel, a carpenter from Ontario, helped to build many pioneer buildings and his sons still live in the district. Another Prince Edward Islander, Armichael Nicholson's son Sam owns the original farm. The Israels also competed strongly for the cordwood market to supply the river boats. At one time they had 1000 cords available. For the second school John Israel and Angus McLean supervised the building and Albert Israel hauled the lumber from the river boats.

Robert George Boyle bought a section of land from George Lee for $50 and two sacks of flour. Mrs. Boyle (Joana Drake) arrived in 1891. Son Arthur Boyle, born in 1893, still farms the home place. John McTavish, after whom the McTavish Road was named, settled in 1884 and Pete Anderson, whose log cabin still stands near the corner of McTavish and Satchell Roads, came in 1883. James Ryder, whose sons, Angus and Harry, now live in Mt. Lehman, arrived from Ontario in 1903. In 1900 Mr. and Mrs. Richard Owen settled on the farm still occupied by Misses Ruth and Lucy Owen and in 1908 the Satchell family purchased property from Neil Craig. The Satchell Road bears their name.

Mt. Lehman's pioneer church, built in 1894, was just completed when a giant fir tree fell on it and it had to be rebuilt. It is still used by the United Church. The first school was established in the 1880's. This was the center of all community activities. The first religious services were held in the school before the building of the church. Teachers who served the school were: Miss Ella Coghlan 1884-7, Miss M. L. Harding 1887, D. W. Sutherland 1887-90, J. R. McLeod 1891-3, John D. McLean 1893-6, Miss L. E. Moss 1896, A. A. McPhail 1896-8, J. F. Hanson 1898-9,

55

Page 55, Where Trails Meet

Norman McLeod 1899.

Three ministers took part in the church services. One was a Methodist, Rev. Manuel, the next a Presbyterian, Dr. Dunn, the next a Church of England, Rev. Hamilton. Both Rev. Hamilton and Dunn served the churches in the area, travelling on horseback. Rev. Hamilton was in the habit of stopping at the Boyle's place and because he was an ardent pipe smoker was accused of starting Mr. Boyle smoking.

Names taken from the Church contribution fund in March 1903 were: Gillis, Nicholson, Leclair, Burgess, Dennison, Larmon, Taylor, Merryfield, Marsh, Craig, McTavish, Ryder, McCallum, Lindsay, Miller, Currie Bros., Alder, Ross, Thompson, Morrison, McGregor, White, Coghlan, Hawkins, Payne, Boyle, McDougall, McEachern, Towlan, Carmichael and King.

The Orange Lodge was built after the lodge was established in Mt. Lehman in 1903. This hall has been available as a community hall right up to the present day. Jubilee School was built in 1898, the first teacher being Miss Grace Marshall. There were 15 students registered.

The Mt. Lehman Road, known as Brewster's Trail, was the first road in the district, and stretched to the border. While most of the provisions came by steamboat some feed was brought in by team from South of the line. Oxen were used by many of the farmers, particularly by those settlers who had come from the East Coast. The Taylor's white oxen were named Tom and Jerry. It is not reported what Dan Nicholson called his oxen when they vanished into the woods after upsetting the sleigh in the snow while supposed to be taking Mrs. Nicholson and Mrs. Gillis to visit the Andersons.

The field of sports played an important part in early pioneering, Lacrosse and Soccer being the most important. Herbert and Ed Taylor were keenly interested in Lacrosse and both played for the New Westminster Salmonbellies. Herb travelled with the All-Star team to the San Francisco World's Fair in 1898. John McTavish, Danny Nicholson, Clarence Marsh and others were great Soccer enthusiasts and the Highland United Football team was unbeatable in the early days.

With roads being developed on the top of the mountain area less use of the steamboats became apparent. The end of the river boat era was near. The Old Yale Road was being used regularly and good contact was made with it for freight and passenger travel. The steamboats, however, met competition for considerable time since they could haul lumber and grain more cheaply. Small fruits and produce were now grown abundantly and shipped to New Westminster market, butter and eggs, etc., and the demand exceeded the supply. Fruit orchards had heavy yields and enjoyed the local market for many years finally losing out to the

56

Page 56, Where Trails Meet

Okanagan Valley.

When construction commenced in 1909 on the B.C. Electric right of way Miller decided to move his store to be near the tram. To move a large building 50 years ago was quite a task. Burton Taylor hewed the moving timbers from trees on the Israel property and by use of a capstan literally wound the building on greased logs the half mile to the new site. It took some considerable time to move and necessitated business being done along the way from day to day.

*   *   *

Page 57, Where Trails Meet

Appendix 3

THE STORY OF MOUNT LEHMAN CHURCH

By Gordon Taylor, 2021

I have reviewed the archival materials of the Mount Lehman United Church, given to me by the current board chair. The materials consist of some material from the head office of the Presbyterian Church of British Columbia, dated 1914, as well as notes of my grandmother, Dorothy Taylor, undated, notes of Hugh McDonald church secretary-treasurer, dated 1937, and finally, edited notes of Lucy and Ruth Owen, Mount Lehman pioneers, contained in a chapter on Mount Lehman - from a book found in the Reach Gallery, Abbotsford, called "The Heart of the Fraser Valley". From these notes I have gleaned an understanding of the establishment of our church, which, incidentally, I have attended since 1949.

Mount Lehman School opened in 1884, and was initially used as a place of worship as well, but notes I have read indicate that worship started in local homes even before the school was established. I believe services held in Mount Lehman School were officiated over by several religious denomination, likely including Methodists, Church of England, and Presbyterian. Dr. A. Dunn, in his "History of Presbyterianism in B.C.", quoted by the 1914 Presbyterian church materials, mentions Mount Lehman, and says he had visited pioneers there as early as 1885. The Presbyterian Church head office records indicate that in 1888, the Mount Lehman "mission" of the Presbyterian church was established. Initially the mission was affiliated with other Presbyterian congregations on the north side of the Fraser River. Intermittent supply of Presbyterian ministers followed until 1896, when Mount Lehman was organized as a Presbyterian congregation upon the completion of the church building, the land for which, I presume, was registered in the name of the Presbyterian Church. I recently obtained a copy of the book The Heart of the Fraser Valley, mentioned above, which contains a chapter on Mount Lehman, and which says that the church, from its opening in 1896, until 1903, was known as the "Union Church". The church, land for which was donated by Mr. A. McCallum, had accommodation for 80 worshippers, and was dedicated by Dr. Alexander Dunn on March 15, 1896. After the building and dedication of the church in 1896, it remained a community church, according to my grandmother's notes, with preaching alternating each week between Presbyterian, Methodist and Church of England ministers until in 1903, notes were left on the pulpit for each of the Methodist and Church of England ministers, saying "your services are no longer required", whereupon the church became solely Presbyterian until the vote on joining the United Church of Canada in 1925.

I have read that the church construction was started about 1894, with all volunteer labour being supplied by the congregation, including hand hewing of the support beams by Burton Taylor. However, when the construction was nearing completion, a large tree fell on the church, necessitating rebuilding of a large part of the church. This is why the actual opening and dedication of the church did not occur until 1896. It is interesting to note that the milestone year for the celebration of the church history seems to have varied between 1894, which was probably the year of the start of construction, and 1896, which was the actual dedication year.

During Rev. Gilham's tenure, about 1903, a pulpit was built and installed by parishioner Burgess. In 1910, the responsibility of providing services at Mission and Silverdale were discontinued by the Presbyterian Church head office, and instead Pine Grove and Glenmore were substituted, under the ministry of Mr. J. C. Alder. Also under Mr. Alder's watch a manse site was purchased adjoining the north side of the church lot. The owner of the lot, Mr. McCallum, sold the lot to the church for $100, and donated $10, leaving $90 to be raised by donations. To actually build the manse, four church members donated $10 each, with each one also giving five days work. In addition to donation of labour, lumber was generously donated by the Abbotsford Lumber Co. and Cook's Mill of Mount Lehman donated mill services. Mr. and Mrs. Alder were the first ministers to reside in the manse in 1913.

The next minister, Mr. Reid, who arrived in 1913, arranged the building of a horse shed, for the convenience of those driving to church. Mr. Reid also brought with him a supply of fruit trees, which he planted on the manse grounds. My grandmother's notes also indicate that the minsters relied on members of the congregation for transportation, as none owned a car (which also involved the church members driving the minister to and from the partner churches,) but one minister took it upon himself to purchase his own car, which he stored in the horse shed behind the church. I remember playing in this shed, during the 1950s and 1960s; it also had a hayloft, as I recall. I also recall being invited over to the manse during Rev. Manderson's term, as the minister's daughter was in my class at Mount Lehman School.

During a subsequent minster's term about 1917, Mr. Mitchell organized a new foundation to be placed under the church, and also the building of a verandah to be added to the manse. Mr. Oswald followed Mr. Mitchell, and he was instrumental in having a "Memorial Hall" built, adjoining the east wall of the church, (the area we currently call the church kitchen). Former minster Rev. Reid made a substantial donation to the Memorial Hall in memory of his son Willie, who died in Flanders Fields during World War I. In 1921, Mrs. N. Carter (this is Lizzie Taylor's sister) presented the congregation with a communion set, in memory of her husband, Norton Carter, who died in 1916 while serving Canada overseas. This is the communion set that is still used today.

On March 15, 1921, the 25th anniversary of the opening of the church was held in the Orange Hall, well attended by the community and many past ministers including Rev. Wm Reid, Rev. C. McDiarmid, Mr. Douglas, Mr. J.C. Alder and Mr. Oswald.

In 1925, Rev. Oswald supervised a vote at the church as to whether the church should become part of the United Church of Canada, which combined many Methodist, Congregational, Presbyterian and Union churches into the fold. The move in Mount Lehman was not without controversy, especially with some of the Presbyterian members of the congregation. A substantial Presbyterian contingent left the Mount Lehman congregation, and started up a new Presbyterian Church at the corner of Harris and Mount Lehman Roads, to be called "Dunn Memorial Presbyterian Church". The rift between the new Presbyterian church and Mount Lehman United Church was particularly deep, I am told, with boyfreinds not being able to continue relationship with girlfriends, for example, and when a Mount Lehman parishioner went over to a Presbyterian household to collect the communion set, it was thrown out the door unceremoniously onto the lawn.

So the Mount Lehman United Church carried on, and does so to this day. In 1927, a new organ was purchased by the Ladies Aid group, with Mr. A. Smith donating $50 towards its purchase. This is the organ which to this day sits in the narthex of the church, welcoming visitors. It is also the organ upon which many organists, including my grandmother (for many years) and me, for about 5 years, played for the congregation.

In 1928, Rev. Robert Moses became the minister; he was responsible for an era which made a number of improvements, including a wooden tennis court (which my grandmother told me she played upon), a new porch to the front of the church, and a concrete walk and notice board. Also in that year, under the leadership of Miss Gwladys Forrester (my grandmother's sister), the Girls' Auxilliary leader, a collection plate was purchased. As well, a christening bowl was purchased with funds from the Sunday school birthday box, and the first baby of Mr. and Mrs. James Threlfall was the first to be christened using this bowl. It is said that Mr. Moses also led a fine group of boys which he took to the seaside for a week each summer; one of whom, Hubert Farber, attended the Older Boys Parliament of British Columbia. I also attended Older Boys Parliament, for many years, representing the church, and was elected Premier in 1970.

Over the years, Mount Lehman ministers of our church were also responsible for preaching at partner charges; for example in 1936, then minister Rev. Donaldson preached at Clayburn every Sunday morning, at Poplar in the afternoon and at Mount Lehman in the evening. This must have been a gruelling schedule for the minister. (Another partner charge gratefully appreciated by our congregation was that with Aldergrove United, which association lasted for thirty years, from about 1960-1990).

Carrying on with 1930s notes, our Sunday school had 40 pupils under the leadership of Mrs. Gamsby and Mrs. L. Steward, with other teachers Mrs. Forrester (my great-grandmother), Mrs. Farber, Mrs. Simpson and Sonia Savitsky. There was also a Ladies Aid group which met every month, and also a sewing circle which met once a month at the home of one of its members.

Then there is this note in Mr. McDonald's history: "It affords me a great pleasure at this time to state that we still have one of the oldest settlers with us, Mrs. Anna Taylor, who celebrated her one-hundredth birthday on October 4, 1937, with her three sons and their families. As well, the Reeve, George Cruikshank and the municipal staff presented her with a birthday cake and a bouquet of flowers. Mrs. Taylor never lost that pioneering spirit. In her conversations even today, she will refer to things which took place in her early life." This quote refers to my great-great grandmother.

To summarize, some of the parishioners spoken of by Mr. Hugh McDonald in his 1937 history, other than those already mentioned:

Mr. Carmichael, Mr. Neil Craig, Mr. T. Dennison, Mr. Burgess, J. Dennison, A. Nicholson, D. Nicholson, W. Merryfield, A. Gillis, Mr. S. Larmon, Mrs. Bates, Mr. and Mrs. MacDougald, Mrs. Bernice McDonald (organist for 15 years), H. McDonald, Mrs. Lillian Farber, James Simpson (a former Reeve of Matsqui), J. E. Israel, Mrs. H. McDonald, Elizabeth Forrester (my great grandmother).

It is not my intention, in this story, to trace the history of our church up to the present, although the church is still a vital part of our community. My purpose in this story is to show the contribution and dedication to this church of many pioneer families, including my own.

Appendix 4

HISTORY OF MOUNT LEHMAN LIBRARY

By Dorothy Taylor

There has been a continuous library service in Mount Lehman since 1930. In fact, since about 1928, numerous meetings in the Fraser Valley took place with Dr. Helen Stewart, a representative of the Carnegie Foundation, and volunteers interested in a library in Mount Lehman. As a result of those meetings, a bookmobile first visited Mount Lehman in 1930, on a weekly basis.

Volunteers of the library in Mount Lehman decided that a deposit library would be more satisfactory than a bookmobile. At the time, there was a small shop (Pete Laurenti's Boots, Shoes and Harness General Repairs and Butcher Shop) on Mount Lehman Road, next to the general store, where a small space was made available for the library on two afternoons per week. This space served for some time, until the building was sold.

The general store then offered a small storeroom at the rear, with a table and chair for the custodian, some shelves for about 100-150 books (adult and children), a long bench for customers to rest, and a small airtight heater with donated wood for heat. This was the library until 1947, when MacAskills' store burned down. The book-mobile came again while we looked for other library space.

The Mount Lehman Credit Union had a new building and offered library space in their committee room, where the library continued every Wednesday and Saturday afternoons until 1958, when the Credit Union required the space. Then the Army Navy and Air Force Veterans Club offered the library the use of a small room within its building. The club members built shelves, and supplied a desk and chairs. This room was the largest and most used library to date- the only drawback was where the building was situated, namely not on Mount Lehman Road.

After negotiations with Matsqui Municipal Council, a new library building was built beside Mount Lehman Post Office. The library moved into the new building on June 15, 1974, and the volunteers had finally gained their objective- a public library in Mount Lehman. Despite a minor setback when the building was damaged by fire in 1987, it was re-opened later that year, and has been enjoyed by the book lovers of Mount Lehman ever since.

The library would like to thank former volunteers for their work - they are:

Mrs. E. Forrester
Mrs. M Gamsby
Mr. C. Savitsky
Miss Lucy Owen
Mrs. Dorothy Taylor
Ms. Mary-Elisabeth Stadnyk.

Appendix 5

HISTORY OF MATSQUI UNIT 315, ARMY, NAVY AND AIR FORCE VETERANS IN CANADA

By Douglas Grant Burton Taylor

Following World War I, a branch of the Great War Veterans Association was formed in Mount Lehman. It was formed about 1920, and met at the Orange Hall. Prominent members were Fred Carter (Boer War and W.W.I), Alfred Tucker (W.W.I), J. P. Carr (W.W.I), James Simpson (W.W.I), Cecil Gibson (M.M. and Bar,(W.W.I), S. Leslie Brice (W.W.I)-Secretary, Murdoch Gillis (D.C.M. (W.W.I) and John Gray (W.W.I).

About 1930, the Association amalgamated with the Matsqui-Sumas-Abbotsford Branch 15 of the Royal Canadian Legion.

A crisis in Mount Lehman during the late 1940s changed the veterans' loyalties. Someone behind the scenes was advocating closing the Mount Lehman Post Office, and moving it to Clearbrook. This was vociferously opposed by the whole Mount Lehman community, and also by the veterans' group. The veterans, led by Fred Carter, presented a resolution to the MSA Branch of the Royal Canadian Legion, asking for support for the retention of the Mount Lehman

Post Office. The Legion refused its support. This refusal infuriated the Mount Lehman veterans, who then disassociated themselves from the Legion group, and sought the formation of a new veterans group. The W.W.I veterans felt that they had made a mistake by amalgamation of the old Great War Veterans' Association with the Legion, who felt they only had an interest in the downtown village area of Abbotsford.

Veterans were solicited to obtain a charter of the Army, Navy and Air Force Veterans in Canada, the oldest veterans organization in Canada, established in 1840.

Charter members were: Clarence Emery, Cecil Gibson, Robert C. Smith, Lee Spreeman, Bert James, Gordon McDonald, Wm. Scott, John Tucker, Harold Black, Robert Merritt, Angus Ryder, L. W. Davis, Fergie Stratton, Joe Langron, Wes Coles, A. A. Holden, C. W. Marsh, P. W. McCormick, L. W. Stewart, J. H. Gray, James Simpson, Leonard S. Philps, Fred Carter, Cecil Grinsted, R. McConachie, Gene Palmer, Bert Anderson, Bruce Stewart, Mel Glover, Sandy Purver, P. McConachie, Ron Grinsted, Wm. Lucas, John Carter, Doug Taylor, George Baloc, Muriel Israel, James Taylor and Howard Israel.

The new Charter gave its jursidiction as the District of Matsqui. After leasing the Orange Hall for ten years, in 1961 the Club purchased a heritage wartime building at Abbotsford Airport, and moved it to a site on McNeil Road, Mount Lehman, which was donated by the McNeil and Taylor families.

The early years of the Army and Navy Club were a struggle. The Club had little money, so five of the club members signed a note at the bank, and borrowed $5,000. This money was used to move the new building from Abbotsford Airport, to a new foundation located on McNeil Road. The clubrooms were opened on November 4, 1961.

The new clubrooms housed the unit and its many functions, and at the same time, Matsqui Unit has made the hall available to the community at large, at reasonable rental rates.

The veterans were successful in establishing their new Club premises, and the community was successful in retaining the Mount Lehman Post Office.

In 1991, Unit 315 commenced a new project; since Matsqui District had no cenotaph, Club members launched a fund-raising campaign, so that a new cenotaph would be built to the memory of those who had given their lives in the service of Canada's military - a lasting tribute - lest we forget. The cenotaph was dedicated in 1992.

Appendix 6

EULOGY FOR DOUGLAS GRANT BURTON TAYLOR

Given at his Funeral Service by Gordon Douglas Taylor, on Friday, February 27, 1998 at Mount Lehman United Church

My name is Gordon Taylor, Doug's eldest son. On behalf of our family, I would like to thank you for coming today to pay your kind respects to the memory of my father.

On February 22, 1998 the olympic torch was extinguished at Nagano, Japan, ending the winter games. It seemed ironic to me at the time that it should also be the day that Dad passed away. You could say that Dad's life was a lot like the olympics. In fact, when you hear my story here today, you might well say that his life could really have been called the "Mount Lehman Olympics". In effect, his torch was lit in 1924, when he was born in what was then Matsqui Municipality. His great-grandparents had arrived here from Nova Scotia in 1887, they had helped to build this church in 1894, and he was raised on the family farm located a very short distance from where we are now, on Taylor Road. The first part of his life was really his olympic training period, before he really started going for gold.

Dad was the younger of two boys born to Buster and Dorothy Taylor. His dad Buster predeceased him in 1966. His mother Dorothy is here today and resides up the road at Val Haven home. Like his father and his brother, Dad attended Mount Lehman Elementary school, as did I and my brothers and sister, and my children - four generations of our family have attended that school, the land for which was donated for that purpose by our family. Then he attended Phillip Sheffield High School, where he distinguished himself academically, and was particularly artistic, especially in the area of cartooning and sketching. As was common with Canadian boys growing up in the war years, he couldn't wait to sign up, but his father made him wait until he turned 18. He then signed up, joined the Royal Canadian Air Force, and service in various places in Canada, including St. Thomas, Ontario, Pat Bay and Tofino, B.C. and Rivier du Loop, Quebec. He was an air frame mechanic, repairing and maintaining the aircraft then constructed of fabric and wood.

After he was discharged, he decided to work with his brother Jim. They started out in the feed business, offloading boxcars at a siding near Ross Road and Harris. Later they started a general merchants business in 1945, located where his insurance office is now established. They sold feed, groceries, hardware, and when his father Buster joined the partnership, they added gas pumps and an automotive repair shop. In 1949, Dad bought an existing insurance business from an old gent in Matsqui Prairie, and he started selling residential and private auto insurance.

Dad married my mother in 1947, and they raised their family of four children three doors from this church, where we lived until they built their "new" house in 1969. You have to understand the nature of the family business in those days - we delivered feed, groceries and barrels of gas in our old flat-deck truck, and from the time I was old enough to drive, I was off delivering to all the old Mount Lehman pioneer families who, even at that time, our family had known for several generations. Families like the Boyles on Satchell Road, the McCormicks, the Marshes, the Owens - Dad introduced me to them all and encouraged me to listen to their stories of Mount Lehman history - it was vitally important to him that each customer be treated with the utmost respect, so that is how my training in dealing with the public got started. Dad's philosophy was that there was no time, day or night, that was too late or inconvenient for him, if a customer needed something from the store. Serving the community in business and community work was more important to him than getting rich. That carried on to his other careers, including municipal politics.

I guess Dad had always been interested in politics, even before kids came along, but he always instilled in us his interest in honest politics. Along with that came a lot of hard work, which he was willing to do. He was active in the Progressive Conservative party in the 50s, and was defeated by Harold Hicks at the nominating convention by 3 votes, otherwise he would have been the M.P. for Fraser Valley during the Diefenbaker sweep of 1957. Later he ran as the provincial conservative candidate in two provincial general elections. He was never deterred by the fact that he might be the underdog in a campaign - in fact that made him work more furiously. He took a personal stand on issues, and stuck by it through thick and thin. One of the proudest moments in my life occurred in 1967, when both Dad and I attended the Progressive Conservative party Leadership convention in Toronto's Maple Leaf Gardens, he as a regular delegate and I as a youth delegate. We decided to support Dief the Chief, and when he lost after several ballots, we switched to Roblin. You all know what happended - Stanfield won, but neither he nor I ever second-guessed our decisions. You will find, to this day, a picture of Dief on the wall in his insurance office. It was about this time in his children's eyes that we realized that, in the olympic scheme of things, he was entering medal competition.

Dad harboured certain minor regrets about not continuing his education after his discharge from the Air Force. I think that is why he told me, when in Grade 9, that I should go into law. He also encouraged me to go to what was then the Older Boys Parliament of British Columbia. He encouraged that education for me and assisted me financially all the way through. Similarly, he helped my sister through her university education, to become a teacher. In the case of my two brothers, I think he came to the conclusion that they were not trainable by anyone else but him, so he brought them into his insurance business, causing that business to flourish. His theory seemed to be to encourage a person again and again, and never let any small setback be a discouragement from attaining a goal. His home and help were always open to us, and quite frankly, I leaned on him for help, both personally and in my business, up to the week of his death. We children all helped him and Mum and each other, and unlike most families these days, we always lived within 2 minutes of each other.

His family always helped him in politics. I met my wife Sharon, for instance, while we were putting brochures on car windows when he ran the first time for the mayor's office, the time he beat Spud by 13 votes. He just loved municipal politics and there was no job too big or too small. One day he would be greeting Queen Elizabeth or installing the Royal Westminster Regiment with the freedom of the city; the next day he would be out checking a taxpayer's flooded basement, later stopping to work at the insurance office, and then when he got home he would feed his cattle. His terms of office saw

the building of Sevenoaks Shopping Centre, and many improvements in the municipality of Matsqui, including the installing of a
major water system. He not only had visions for municipal development, but he followed them through. Mount Lehman benefitted
greatly from his work, from his finding a permanent home for the
Mt. Lehman Library to the setup of the Mt. Lehman Fire Hall, where
he also served as a volunteer fireman for 14 years. Prior to entering municipal politics, he jointly with Edwin Olund, developed the
Merryfield Avenue subdivision, in the days when the corner lots
sold for $2,000.

He continued up to the last to contribute to the community. The
Community Association of Mount Lehman in late 1997 appointed
him to a City of Abbotsford committee to suggest ideas to improve
rural areas. I have his note - it will be no surprise to you to know he
had some great new ideas. Also, he on his own petitioned council
and Canada Post, and only a few weeks before his death succeeded
in restoring our ability to use Mount Lehman again legally as our
address for the receipt of mail.

He had a vast appetite for local history. People for miles around
would come to him to track down long lost relatives or to ask questions about early Mount Lehman history, and he would spend hours
answering questions, digging out documents, doing research. He
continued working on our Taylor family history when non-one in
our family could bear to listen any more. But do you know what
happened in 1995 - he tracked down our long lost relatives in Nova
Scotia who were directly related to our family who first can to Mt.
Lehman, and I am pleased to say that finally got stung with the
same bug. In the summer of 1997, Mum and Dad and Sharon and I
attended a family reunion in Nova Scotia and met for the first time
80 direct or indirect relatives previously unknown. He succeeded in

tracking our branch of the Taylor family back to 1660 in Connecticut. He never gave up. Using my olympic medal example, he was really in serious contention. In fact, 1997 was probably the most fun year of our whole family's life with Mum and Dad. In addition to our Nova Scotia trip, our yearly family fishing trip was turned into a party to celebrate their 50th wedding anniversary, where they got to visit with all their family, they went to Mexico with Grant and Carol, we went to Loon Lake with them many times, and they went to Saskatchewan to help celebrate John and Ann Wall's 50th wedding anniversary. Mexico was definitely their favourite spot, and they just returned in January 1998 from their 71st trip there.

I won't mention in detail all the other organizations in which he was active - most of them are represented here today - but they were the Army, Navy and Air Force Veterans here in Mount Lehman - he was a charter member. The Masonic Lodge. The Loyal Orange Lodge. MSA Pioneers' Association. MSA Minor Hockey Association. He volunteered as a Matsqui Police auxiliary member at one time, and later in life became chairman of the police commission - he even carried in his wallet a Matsqui Police badge given to him upon leaving politics. He also served with the Royal Westminster Regiment for many years, rising to the rank of Captain.

Have you noticed that I haven't said yet that he entered the medals round? That's because I have saved the best for last. The area where he had hundreds of medals around his neck by the day he died was his relationship with each and every member of his family and his friends. A day wouldn't go by where he wouldn't say to me "I wonder what Rose is doing today, I better call her", or "what are Karen and Ryan up to tonight?" Or "Come on over, Britney's here and we get to babysit all night". This is where he hit the gold for us, and probably for you.

We all feel we had so much unfinished business with him, each for our own selfish reasons, but you know he lived a fantastic life, and achieved most of the things he would have wanted, and aside from being taken from us far too early, he went the way he would have wanted if he knew his time was up. I'm sure he would direct us to that poem well loved by him of Lieut.-Col. John McCrae, if he knew we were all here today, mourning his loss, the poem that he used when he spoke to elementary students about the meaning of Remembrance Day … you know the one that starts "In Flanders fields, the poppies blow, between the crosses row on row... I think he would tell us to skip a few lines in the poem to the part that reads "Take up our quarrel with the foe; to you from failing hands we throw the torch; be yours to hold it high. If ye break faith with us who die, We shall not sleep, though poppies grow In Flanders Fields".

The Mount Lehman olympian has now relayed the torch to you and me, to take over where he left off and to carry it forward. It will be made easier by following the example he has set for us.

-Thanks, Dad.

Printed in Canada